ASCD MEMBER BOOK

Many ASCD members received this book as a
member benefit upon its initial release.

Learn more at: **www.ascd.org/memberbooks**

101 Strategies to Make Academic Vocabulary Stick

MARILEE SPRENGER

ASCD | ALEXANDRIA, VIRGINIA

1703 N. Beauregard St. • Alexandria, VA 22311-1714 USA
Phone: 800-933-2723 or 703-578-9600 • Fax: 703-575-5400
Website: www.ascd.org • E-mail: member@ascd.org
Author guidelines: www.ascd.org/write

Deborah S. Delisle, *Executive Director;* Robert D. Clouse, *Managing Director, Digital Content & Publications;* Stefani Roth, *Publisher;* Genny Ostertag, *Director, Content Acquisitions;* Carol Collins, *Senior Acquisitions Editor;* Julie Houtz, Director, *Book Editing & Production;* Miriam Calderone, *Editor;* Donald Ely, *Senior Graphic Designer;* Mike Kalyan, *Manager, Production Services;* Cynthia Stock, *Production Designer;* Kelly Marshall, *Senior Production Specialist*

All web links in this book are correct as of the publication date below but may have become inactive or otherwise modified since that time. If you notice a deactivated or changed link, please e-mail books@ascd.org with the words "Link Update" in the subject line. In your message, please specify the web link, the book title, and the page number on which the link appears.

PAPERBACK ISBN: 978-1-4166-2310-6   ASCD product #117022
PDF E-BOOK ISBN: 978-1-4166-2312-0; see Books in Print for other formats.

Quantity discounts: 10–49, 10%; 50+, 15%; 1,000+, special discounts (e-mail programteam@ascd.org or call 800-933-2723, ext. 5773, or 703-575-5773). For desk copies, go to www.ascd.org/deskcopy.

ASCD Member Book No. FY17-4B (Jan. 2017 PS). Member books mail to Premium (P), Select (S), and Institutional Plus (I+) members on this schedule: Jan, PSI+; Feb, P; Apr, PSI+; May, P; Jul, PSI+; Aug, P; Sep, PSI+; Nov, PSI+; Dec, P. For details, see www.ascd.org/membership and www.ascd.org/memberbooks.

Library of Congress Cataloging-in-Publication Data

Names: Sprenger, Marilee, 1949–
Title: 101 strategies to make academic vocabulary stick / Marilee Sprenger.
Other titles: One hundred and one strategies to make academic vocabulary stick
Description: Alexandria, Virginia : ASCD, 2017. | Includes bibliographical
    references and index.
Identifiers: LCCN 2016041976 (print) | LCCN 2016042917 (ebook) | ISBN
    9781416623106 (pbk.) | ISBN 9781416623120 (PDF)
Subjects: LCSH: Vocabulary—Study and teaching—United States.
Classification: LCC LB1574.5 .S723 2016 (print) | LCC LB1574.5 (ebook) | DDC
    372.44—dc23
LC record available at https://lccn.loc.gov/2016041976

23 22 21 20 19 18 17   1 2 3 4 5 6 7 8 9 10 11 12

For all of the students who inspired me,
and to the teachers who work hard every day to
help them upgrade their vocabularies.

Acknowledgments

This book contains strategies that have both research and anecdotal evidence supporting them. There are so many experts to thank, but I will mention just a few whose work inspired me. To Robert Marzano, Michael Graves, Eric Jensen, Isabel Beck, Margaret McKeown, Linda Kucan, Camille Blachowicz, Peter Fisher, Donna Ogle, and Susan Watts Taffe: thank you all for your outstanding work.

Special thanks to Carol Collins, Stefani Roth, and the ASCD book acquisitions team who believe in this work. Thank you for your guidance and friendship. Much gratitude goes to Miriam Calderone, ASCD editor, who worked hard to make the information in this book easy to understand and apply. Thanks for making me sound good!

If it weren't for my family—Scott, Josh, Marnie, Amy, Matt, Jack, Emmie, Maeven, Mia, Charlie, and Vivi—this book would have been done *sooner,* but they are all too much fun not to hang out with! I love you all.

Introduction
Addressing Word Poverty

Far too many students come to school with small vocabularies. This is a big deal: the size of a child's vocabulary is an accurate predictor of academic achievement and even upward mobility over the course of a lifetime (Hirsch, 2013). Children's vocabulary acquisition is affected by numerous factors, including the number of words exchanged in the home environment, the quality of those words, language spoken in the home, the number of books that have been read to a child, and the amount of time spent in quality conversations. Whichever factors contribute to what I refer to as "word poverty," it is clear that educators across all content areas and grade levels need to provide an enriched environment and implement a broad repertoire of strategies that will immerse all our students in words.

My first vocabulary book, *Teaching the Critical Vocabulary of the Common Core* (2013), focused on 55 high-frequency words used in most standards, including the Common Core standards, and aimed to teach students the vocabulary used on most standardized achievement tests. My motivation for writing that book stemmed from research (Tileston, 2011) estimating that 85 percent of achievement test scores are based on the language used in the standards. At-risk students, including students of low socioeconomic status (SES) and English language learners (ELLs), have a particular need to learn these words in ways that meet their specific learning requirements. *Teaching the Critical Vocabulary of the Common Core* addressed that need.

As teachers recognized the importance of teaching those 55 critical words and began adopting new vocabulary strategies, the need for even more strategies to teach even more words became apparent.

Throughout their elementary and secondary school careers, students will learn about 50,000 words (Nagy & Anderson, 1984; Nagy & Herman, 1987; White, Graves, & Slater, 1990), averaging 3,000–4,000 words each year, most through implicit learning. This *implicit learning* is nonconscious and usually happens by reading, being read to, and engaging in high-quality conversations. In addition, teachers should be teaching about 300 *academic words* through direct instruction. The 300-word target comes to an average of about 60 words for each content area, although many academic words overlap areas: for example, we *summarize* in social studies, science, and English. Many schools create lists for each grade level based on the vocabulary of the standards and their curriculum.

The importance of teaching these words cannot be overstated. According to Susan B. Neuman, a professor in educational studies specializing in early literacy development, "[Vocabulary has] been one of the most resistant-to-change skills in early literacy. Generally, children come into school with vocabulary at one point and leave with vocabulary at the same point" (quoted in Sparks, 2013).

This goal is particularly important for English language learners and students who come from low-SES homes. Low socioeconomic status can adversely affect the vocabularies and literacy skills of both native speakers of English and English language learners. Beyond this factor, students who are English language learners generally have smaller English vocabularies. One of the key factors in ELLs' vocabulary acquisition in English, however, is their vocabulary acquisition in their primary language. Those who have a larger word bank in their native language can use those meanings and spellings to help them infer meanings of new English words (Graves, August, & Mancilla-Martinez, 2013). For instance, using *cognates*—words that have similar spellings and meanings in two languages—for Spanish-speaking students is extremely effective because up to 40 percent of all English words have a Spanish cognate. Pointing out words with cognates as you read aloud, asking students to identify cognates in their own reading, and creating a cognate word wall are three possible strategies for teaching cognates.

To change future outcomes of vocabulary learning and close these gaps, teachers need both professional development in teaching vocabulary and vocabulary strategies at their fingertips. Many teachers have not had adequate preparation for explicitly teaching vocabulary and resort to Internet searches and professional books for novel, engaging strategies. These strategies are everywhere, but they are not located in one place, and they vary in effectiveness—which is where this book comes in.

TIER 2 WORDS: THEIR IMPORTANCE

So what, exactly, are these 300 academic words that must be explicitly taught? Let's back up a bit.

There are three tiers of vocabulary that encompass all the words our students can learn. Tier 1 includes basic vocabulary, Tier 2 includes high-frequency academic vocabulary, and Tier 3 includes low-frequency specialized vocabulary.

Tier 1 words are those words used in everyday speech that students generally have in their long-term memories, such as *table, clock, food, run, ride, drive,* and so on. Tier 3 words are those that are specific to content areas. For instance, *meiosis* is used in science and generally not in other subjects. It is good to teach some Tier 3 words, but they are often defined in the text in which they appear.

Tier 2 words are those that I call "everybody's words." These vocabulary words often have multiple meanings in different contexts, appear frequently in written sources across the content areas but are not discipline-specific, and are considered academic words. A word like *letter* is a Tier 2 word with multiple meanings; it can mean a symbol that represents a sound or a way of communicating with someone. *Analyze* is a Tier 2 word that is used across the content areas; students are asked to analyze stories, musical selections, artwork, math problems, and so on. As *academic words,* Tier 2 words are used primarily in academic texts and classrooms and are not likely to be encountered by students in casual conversations.

Although Tiers 1 and 3 are important, Tier 2 words are the most necessary to teach explicitly (Beck, McKeown, & Kucan, 2013). Much research (Blachowicz, Fisher, Ogle, & Taffe, 2013; Marzano, 2004) stresses the importance of students mastering a significant body of Tier 2 words and urges teachers to use more academic terms in the classroom for discussion and personal dialogue. So why, if these words are so important, are most of us not teaching them to our students? There are several reasons:

- We tend to assume that if we know a word, so does everyone else.
- When a word is found across the content areas, we assume that some other teacher has taught it.
- We are under the impression that students will discover words for themselves using a dictionary or the Internet.
- We don't have time to teach vocabulary. There are too many standards, so we choose those that are visible to us, that make sense to our own brains, and with which we are comfortable.

Recently, however, following the lead of the grade-level expectations laid out by the Common Core and state standards in both Common Core and non–Common Core states, the testing companies (PARCC, SBA, ACT, SAT, NWEA, ACT Aspire) have become aware that vocabulary is not an add-on for which students are solely responsible and that we can ignore. In fact, vocabulary may be the most important content that we teach. The link among vocabulary, reading, writing, speaking, and listening is becoming increasingly clear, and academic vocabulary is frequently referenced (Beck et al., 2013; Marzano, 2004) as a critical element in reading comprehension and academic achievement.

These academic words are the focus of the strategies in this book. In the pages that follow, you'll find an array of strategies for teaching the hundreds of words that students will need in school and beyond.

THE ROLE OF MEMORY AND THE ORGANIZATION OF THIS BOOK

If we want to get words into long-term memory and make them stick, we need to keep some fundamentals in mind. Most words need to be processed multiple times and in various ways to make them permanent. In *Teaching the Critical Vocabulary of the Common Core*, I shared strategies that would get those critical words quickly into *nonmotor procedural memory*, which I often refer to as *automatic memory*. Those 55 words are so crucial for student assessments that I believed it best to teach many of them the same way we teach decoding skills, fluency, and even multiplication: repetition, repetition, repetition. In this context, repetition doesn't mean rote drill; rather, this method incorporates elaborate rehearsals that engage all the senses in novel, fun ways.

For the Tier 2 words covered in this book, I have taken a slightly different tack. The emphasis is on first getting words into semantic long-term memory before eventually getting them into nonmotor procedural memory (again, also known as automatic memory). As a strong proponent of brain-compatible teaching and differentiation, I have selected strategies that will appeal to different levels of readiness and will provide a pathway in the brain to create strong memories (Gallagher, 2014). Almost all of the strategies can be used at all grade levels. Here's how the book is organized.

In Chapter 1, I share the background research on vocabulary and memory, citing studies that point to a vocabulary pathway in the brain and explaining the memory systems and how vocabulary words are stored in and through them.

Chapters 2, 3, and 4 and their strategies are organized according to the stages of building long-term memories: *encoding*, *storage*, and *retrieval*. In Chapter 2, I share dozens of encoding strategies to introduce new words and begin the memory process. During this stage, it's important to create an atmosphere in which students feel safe to try and fail. Knowing their teachers and classmates believe in them makes a huge difference in how students approach learning. Thus, the strategies in this chapter will help you reach students so that words can more readily be encoded in their brains.

From encoding in Chapter 2, we move to storage in Chapter 3. This stage is when we do elaborate rehearsals to get the words, definitions, visuals, and concepts related to each word stored permanently in the brain. The networks have been laid and made; now it is time to use the new words in multisensory activities that enter the mind through various systems for easier retrieval. Chapter 3 shares rehearsal strategies that help students *recode*, or define vocabulary terms in their own words. From synonyms to sentences, this stage encourages writing that will more clearly define and describe the academic vocabulary.

After the storage stage comes the retrieval stage—the focus of Chapter 4. During this stage, we use review to encourage retrieval of word knowledge and gain the automaticity needed for reading comprehension. *Automaticity* is the ability to read words without conscious decoding and understand them without needing to search one's brain for definitions. Our students cannot afford to use precious working memory space on decoding and figuring out word meanings; they need it for comprehension. Accordingly, to help students gain automaticity, Chapter 4 provides review strategies that will help student practice recalling words and meanings, using the words in speaking and writing, and understanding them in reading. Students will combine several words in sentences, make comparisons among words, and, most important, use the words in natural conversation and daily writing.

I wrap up the book with Chapter 5, which focuses on the intertwined components of assessment and planning. You will find rubrics and sample one- and two-week lesson plans using various strategies included in this book. We'll explore questions like "How long will you study each word?" and "When will you assess?"

GIVING THE GIFT OF VOCABULARY

The release of the Common Core State Standards brought the importance of vocabulary instruction to the fore. Students are beginning to take the next generation of assessments that require higher cognitive demand as based on Webb's Depth of Knowledge and Bloom's Taxonomy. But the importance of expanding our students' Tier 2 vocabulary transcends these assessments: a strong academic vocabulary lays a solid foundation for success in life, just as a small vocabulary is a major disadvantage.

I have thought long and hard about teaching vocabulary at all levels, as I have in my own classrooms. I have studied research, talked to teachers, modeled lessons in classrooms, and compiled a plethora of strategies. Some of the 101 strategies in this book you may already know. Others, perhaps, will be brand-new to you. Some may require a tweak to work with your students. But I urge you not to discount any tools out of hand as either "too young" or "too tough" for your students. Certainly there is a difference between how we work with words in kindergarten and how we do it in 5th grade, but most strategies can be used in various grade levels. I have created an at-a-glance chart that lists all 101 strategies and indicates their approximate grade range as well as which strategies work particularly well for ELLs or low-SES students. You can access this chart at http://www.ascd.org/ASCD/pdf/books/sprenger2017.pdf.

I have no doubt that you will find strategies here to help you teach academic vocabulary in a way that will make it stick. If you are committed to teaching vocabulary and need more strategies to do so, this book is for you. If you teach students who live in poverty, this book is for you. If you have a large population of English language learners, you will find strategies for them, too. We owe this to our students. Let's jump in together.

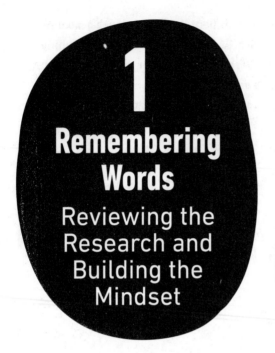

1

Remembering Words

Reviewing the Research and Building the Mindset

I often visit schools where I get to work with exceptional teachers. At one Chicago school, I spent a lot of time in an ESL primary classroom where the teacher, Jacquie Erickson, worked with her students using strategies from my first two vocabulary books, *Teaching the Critical Vocabulary of the Common Core* (2013) and *Vocab Rehab: How Do I Teach Vocabulary Effectively with Limited Time?* (2014). Although I had not specifically created lessons for English language learners, these brain-friendly strategies were effective for these students because they offered varied ways of learning.

For vocabulary instruction to be effective, we must meet students where they are and use strategies that take into account how their brains and memories work. In this chapter, I review some of the research behind how the brain learns and retains new words and explain how to prime students for vocabulary instruction to take hold.

INSIGHTS FROM RESEARCH

We are fortunate to teach in an age that abounds with brain research and memory research. Neuroscientists have been able to map the language pathway and the reading pathway in the brain (Sprenger, 2013). Mapping these pathways has enabled us to learn much more about how the brain acquires new vocabulary.

Some research specifically supports a visual word learning method. Reading and comprehension of words are often associated with an area in the left hemisphere of the brain called the *visual word form area* (Dehaene, 2009). Researchers (Glezer, Kim, Rule, Jiang, & Riesenhuber, 2015) believe that this area is used to store words as pictures, particularly after the words are learned through the familiar "sounding out" process, making good fluency possible.

Professor and researcher Maryann Wolf (2010) explains:

> When reading even a single word, the first milliseconds of the reading circuit are largely devoted to decoding the word's visual information and connecting it to all that we know about the word from its sounds to meanings to syntactic functions. The virtual automaticity of this first set of stages allows us in the next milliseconds to go beyond the decoded text. It is within the next precious milliseconds that we enter a cognitive space where we can connect the decoded information to all that we know and feel. In this latter part of the process of reading, we are given the ability to think new thoughts of our own: the generative core of the reading process.

Most of us are familiar with vocabulary strategies that incorporate visuals, such as pictures, drawings, symbols, and graphic organizers. There's a reason for that. Let me illustrate with a common scenario: you're introduced to someone new, and just seconds later you have forgotten his name—but you remember that he's an artist. This phenomenon is often referred to as the "baker/Baker effect." You may not remember Mrs. Baker's name right after you meet her, but if she is a baker, you'll remember that—probably because you visualized the occupation and have a stronger connection to it. In one study (James, 2004), subjects were shown pictures of people along with their names and occupations. Later, when they were shown the pictures again, younger and older participants alike remembered occupations more than names. For this reason, teaching vocabulary is much more effective when the words are associated with visuals of some kind.

In addition to the visual aspect of vocabulary learning, researchers at King's College in London (López-Barroso et al., 2013) have recently found that the *arcuate fasciculus*—a bundle of axons that connects the two speech centers, *Wernicke's area* and *Broca's area*—is the key to remembering new words.

Wernicke's area is the brain's lexicon of words and their meanings, whereas Broca's area is involved with the articulation of speech. The researchers found that the more myelinated the arcuate fasciculus was—myelination being the process by which axons are covered in *myelin*, a fatty coating that makes nerve impulses move faster and more effectively—the more easily a word was remembered. In addition, articulation of the word helps reinforce the connection between the two speech structures. Therefore, the importance of having students speak new words cannot be overstated. Providing more opportunities for students to repeat a new vocabulary word and then use it when speaking increases the likelihood of their using it again.

It behooves us to approach vocabulary instruction using sound pedagogy that incorporates the conclusions of these research findings, including the use of repetition and reinforcement that strengthen the word connections in the brain. Researcher Michael Graves (2006) devised a four-part plan for teaching vocabulary that provides multiple avenues for learning and incorporates both explicit and implicit modes of learning. His plan includes the following four elements:

1. **A rich language environment.** Students should be immersed in a word-filled world. Some ways teachers can achieve this are by reading with and to students, through direct instruction and discussion of new vocabulary (Moore, Alvermann, & Hinchman, 2000), and by encouraging students to form "book clubs" in which they read and discuss books of their choice. Students should read and write across genres and content areas, and teachers should be sure to provide informational text along with fiction. You will find more ideas for creating a rich, word-filled environment throughout this book.

2. **Focus on individual words.** Teaching individual words is at the heart of increasing vocabularies. Because our student populations are so diverse, a toolbox of strategies is necessary to introduce and rehearse new vocabulary. Teachers should be open to what students need and vary their teaching methods accordingly.

3. **Word-learning strategies.** It's important for students to be able to learn and explore new words independently. Teachers should show students how to use context clues as well as clues from *morphemes* (i.e., the smallest parts of words that contain meaning) to figure out the meaning of new words. Although most

experts agree that generating definitions with students is preferable to using dictionaries as a way of learning vocabulary, teachers should explain to students when a dictionary may be necessary and how to use a thesaurus.

4. Word consciousness. To foster word consciousness, teachers should model an awareness and enjoyment of words and their usefulness. Freely using and playing with words is an important part of building a strong vocabulary.

Baumann, Ware, and Edwards (2007) put Graves's plan to the test by following 5th grade students from diverse backgrounds for one year, during which time the four elements of Graves's approach were incorporated into daily vocabulary lessons. A sampling of the impressive results follows:

• Students' word knowledge grew more than expected as a result of the program's multifaceted approach to vocabulary learning.

• Students who were initially below average in vocabulary knowledge showed greater gains than did classmates who had originally tested above average.

• Writing samples indicated a 36 percent increase in students' word knowledge between fall and spring.

• Low-frequency word use increased by 42 percent between fall and spring.

• Parents' ratings of their children's vocabulary size and appreciation of vocabulary increased between fall and spring.

• Students reported an increase in their interest in reading, writing, and vocabulary from fall to spring.

• Students used more sophisticated and challenging words as the school year progressed.

• Students' attitudes toward learning improved over the school year.

• Students independently used word-learning tools and strategies.

It's clear that Graves is onto something with his four-part plan. But there are still many questions to be answered about teaching and learning vocabulary. For example, how well should words be learned? Must students be able to recognize a word's meaning in multiple contexts and recall its meaning without any triggers or clues? How long are students expected to retain this knowledge? What do we mean when we refer to students "encountering" a word—coming across it in a written text, hearing it in conversation, defining it in a specific teacher-designed exercise, taking the initiative to use it in a sentence, deliberately committing it to memory? All of the above?

The mere presence of these questions indicates that vocabulary is a much more complex and important subject than it's often given credit for. Indeed, it is increasingly clear that vocabulary instruction must not be relegated to an occasional lesson but, rather, should pervade teaching across the curriculum and in all grade levels. As my colleague Mike Fisher writes in *Hacking the Common Core* (2016),

> Friday is not the only day that vocabulary is important, though you'd never guess that was the case in many classrooms in 2016. This practice is still pervasive and it must stop. Vocab is important every day. We don't want to create neural pathways (myelination) in students' brains that hardwire them to care about vocabulary only on Friday. (p. 37)

I agree wholeheartedly with Mike. We have to show our students that vocabulary is important to us, and that it is important every day. We need to teach definitions, pronunciation, relationships among words, strategies for choosing the right word in a given situation, and the kind of deep understanding that will enable our students to write complex sentences using vocabulary words automatically and correctly. How are we going to do this?

INTRODUCING THE FIVE LONG-TERM MEMORY SYSTEMS

Because our ultimate goal is to get vocabulary words into students' long-term memories, let's first look at how long-term memory works. There are actually five long-term memory systems that we can use to get information stored in the brain. Two of these are *explicit*, or *declarative*, systems: semantic and episodic. The other three—motor procedural, nonmotor procedural (automatic), and emotional—are *implicit* memory systems.

Semantic Memory

Semantic memory holds factual information that we have learned from words. Here's how it works: new information enters the brain through the brain stem, goes to the thalamus, and is sent to the hippocampus, which serves as the "file cabinet" for our factual memories. Just as each aisle at the supermarket has a sign telling us which items are on its shelves, the hippocampus holds the signs, or files, for our memories. If incoming sensory information is factual, it will trigger the hippocampus to search its files for matching information. If that existing information connects to the new information, it will be sent to the prefrontal cortex, where working memory will continue to sort and sift the old and the new material. Through prior knowledge or interest, the new information may be added to the old information and form new memories. This process may need to be repeated before permanent memories are formed.

This memory system is a problematic one to use for learning because it takes several repetitions of the learning to cement it into the pathway, and the new learning must be stimulated by associations, comparisons, and similarities to be accessed. Despite the limitations of semantic memory, most of our educational system relies heavily on this system. Textbooks, videos, and lectures are some of the teaching strategies that feed this system.

Episodic Memory

Episodic memory, which relates to locations, people, and events, has also been called *contextual* or *spatial* memory. You are always *somewhere* when you learn something, so that learning may easily be associated with the location. For example, those of us who are old enough to remember the assassination of President Kennedy may ask one another, "Where were you when you found out that JFK had been shot?" For younger people, the 9/11 tragedy is a similar type of memory trigger.

The point is that we all remember some information because it is location-related. The car that you learned to drive in will be easier for you to drive than other cars because you will remember the instructions you received and associate them with this particular car. That's why taking your driving test in a different car tends to make the experience more difficult. Similarly, students who learn information in one room and are tested in another consistently underperform. Episodic memory has an important component that can be called "invisible information." Students have more trouble solving math problems in their English classroom than they do back in math class because the walls, desks, overheads, chalkboards, and even the math teacher provide all kinds of invisible information. The content of the room becomes part of the context of the memory.

Students can improve their semantic and episodic memory through the *recoding* process—that is, by putting information into their own words. This is especially important for students who struggle with a new language, who come from homes with little literacy, or who generally rely more heavily on their surroundings and experiences to build long-term memory. In a study by Szpunar, Chan, and McDermott (2009), three groups of students learned a set of words on computers in five sessions with a 20-minute break between each session. During the breaks, members of group A spent the time as they pleased; members of group B stayed at the computer and went over the words and definitions they had just learned; and members of group C received a blank sheet of paper and were asked to write down everything they remembered from the session. On the unit tests and the final test, group C outscored both of the other groups by about 40 percent. Interestingly, group B did not do much better than group A. This study shows why it is imperative not only to motivate students to attend to the instructional portion of a lesson but also to teach them how to recode and internalize the new information once the lesson is over.

Motor Procedural Memory

The motor procedural memory system is often referred to as "muscle memory." Information found in this system relates to processes that your body engages in and remembers, like riding a bike, skipping rope, roller skating, or driving a car.

The parts of your brain that are responsible for this information in its initial stage are the prefrontal cortex, the parietal cortex, and the cerebellum. For years, it was thought that the cerebellum was used solely for balance and posture, but recent research (Munoz, 2014) suggests that the cerebellum plays a larger, more profound role.

When any procedure becomes routine, it is stored in the motor cortex and cerebellum. So when you first learned to drive, not only was your episodic memory storing factual information, but your motor procedural memory was also activated. Stopping at a red light, hitting your brakes when you see brake lights in front of you, and turning the wheel to avoid collisions are all stored in this system.

The storage of procedural memory within this system has given humans the ability to do two things at once. The fact that we can drive cars and talk on the telephone at the same time (not something I condone!) is evidence of this. Because different areas of the brain are needed for these two functions, they do not fight for brain space or energy.

Nonnmotor Procedural (Automatic) Memory

Nonmotor procedural memory is where any learning that has become automatic for you is stored. The alphabet is stored here, as are Tier 1 words, which are a natural part of our speech. Because retrieval of words from nonmotor procedural memory is automatic, this is the system through which I recommend learning the critical vocabulary found in the Common Core standards. Automatic memory is also where you'd probably find the multiplication tables, your ability to decode words, and lots of songs.

Repeated sets of words are also stored here: think *stop* and *go, black* and *white, up* and *down, in* and *out.* If you practiced learning information on flashcards, that material would also be stored in your automatic memory system.

The use of this system can cause other memory systems to open. For example, imagine that you are listening to the radio, and a song comes on that you haven't heard in a long time. You begin to sing the song and remember that the last time you sang it, you were on your way to the hospital. Now your episodic memory has been triggered. You picture yourself clutching the steering wheel of your blue Oldsmobile as you drove up the hill to this hospital. Now you have activated your procedural memory. As you think about the hospital, you remember why you were there: you were taking your friend to the emergency room. Your semantic system has opened up with this factual information. Suddenly, you feel happy as you recall that you were with your friend when her baby was born: now your emotional memory has been activated.

Emotional Memory

The feeling of happiness evoked by your memory of your friend's baby being born is part of your emotional memory system, which is accessed through your *amygdala*. This brain structure is located in the midbrain next to your hippocampus.

Whereas the hippocampus stores factual information, your amygdala stores emotional information—experiences that made you feel happy, sad, and so on.

Take note: *emotional memory takes precedence over any other kind of memory*. When emotional information enters your brain, your amygdala immediately stores it. If the information calls for strong emotion, especially fear or high stress, the amygdala takes over, triggering a stress response that can help in life-threatening situations but wreak havoc in everyday stressful circumstances, such as taking a test or having a fight with a family member. During such occasions, the release of stress hormones like cortisol can interrupt transmission of information to the brain, making it impossible to think clearly. Daniel Goleman (1998) calls this response a "neural hijacking": at this point, no memory system other than emotional memory has a chance.

Your emotional memory can even be triggered by another memory system and then take over your "logical" mind. For instance, let's say that you need to do some research for a project and decide to see if the local library has a book you need. Suddenly, as you picture the library through your semantic system, you "see" in your mind a librarian who works there whom you cannot tolerate. Your disgust and desire to avoid seeing her at any cost take over your thinking, and you decide to forget looking for that book.

The emotional memory system can also enhance learning. Remember the Baker/baker phenomenon, where the brain remembers an occupation more easily than a name? That changes when the brain makes a direct emotional connection to something important to us. For instance, when you met your future mother-in-law, her name was connected in your brain to a strong existing network, so you were more likely to remember her name. Because emotional memory takes precedence over the other long-term memory systems, teachers would be wise to connect learning to positive emotions, such as joy, pride, and humor.

HELPING STUDENTS GET TO KNOW AND LOVE THEIR BRAINS

To build stronger long-term memories, the strategies in this book appeal to multiple memory systems. In line with this multifaceted approach, it's important also to appeal to our students' many ways of learning, feeling, and being. It is necessary that we teach and nurture the whole child even when we are teaching vocabulary. And the best way to cultivate receptivity to learning is to help students take ownership of it.

In my career, I have witnessed complete turnarounds in students' engagement with text as they learn and "own" new words. Students need to believe that they can learn. Many have spent years hearing, "What's the matter with you?" whenever they misbehave, do something that is not in sync with what caregivers want, or refuse to listen to things that aren't important to them.

I believe that our first job as educators is to show students that there is *nothing* wrong with them. Accordingly, I suggest taking the first week of school or so to teach students about their brains—their *fabulous* brains. Some suggestions for doing so follow.

Explain the five long-term memory systems to students. Give students a rundown of the brain's five long-term memory systems, explaining how each one works and helps students learn in different ways. Helping students to understand their memories will build their confidence and engagement in learning.

Explain about multiple intelligences. Talk about multiple intelligences and learning preferences to give students a chance to see why they might think or learn differently from others. I suggest distributing simple questionnaires to help them understand how they learn best, how they deal with others in the world, and what makes them truly happy. Edutopia is a good source of information on multiple intelligences and provides a short quiz that can be taken online (http://www.edutopia.org/multiple-intelligences-assessment).

Test their memories and ensure success. Many of my students believe that they have terrible memories because they haven't fared well on traditional classroom assessments. This is compounded by their perception that certain classmates seem to remember *everything*! Rather than try to convince them that their memories are as good as their peers', I administer simple memory tests that show them how "good" their brains are.

I begin by "wowing" them with my own amazing memory. First, I ask for a volunteer to be the recorder. Then I list the numbers 1–10 on the board and tell the students that they are going to create a grocery shopping list. After I turn my back so that I cannot see the board, the recorder calls on students in turn to provide an item and its number on the list. For instance, Maeve may say, "Number 3 is toilet paper." The completed list may look like this:

1. Onion
2. Cereal
3. Toilet paper
4. Broccoli
5. Ketchup
6. Spaghetti
7. Chocolate chips
8. Laundry detergent
9. Paper plates
10. Eggs

Next, I ask students in what order they want me to recite the list, and I list the items accordingly. They are invariably impressed by this feat and eager to learn how to do it themselves. So I teach them the rhyming peg system that I use, which assigns each number a rhyming word: 1 = sun, 2 = shoe, 3 = tree, 4 = door, 5 = hive, 6 = sticks, 7 = heaven, 8 = gate, 9 = line, and 10 = hen. Because the pegs rhyme with the numbers, most students just require some practice. I give them time to practice and quiz one another on the pegs.

Once they've got that down, I give them a grocery list—10 items for older students, 5 items for younger students. They must associate each word I give them with the appropriate number without writing anything down. So if I say, "Number 1 is *eggs*," they might visualize the sun (the peg for number 1) as an egg yolk. If number 2 is *watermelon*, they might picture themselves walking around with watermelons for shoes. This kind of strong visualization enables students to remember the words and makes them feel really good about their memories.

I teach memory classes at the college level and for continuing education and have found that adults are exactly like my K–12 students. If I give them memory tests that they can do well on, they feel motivated to continue working on all of their memory issues. We all have memory issues, but our attitude—our mindset— is what makes the difference in terms of how we handle them.

Empower students with a growth mindset. Students need, as Carol Dweck's (2007) research suggests, a *growth mindset*. Do keep in mind that, as she argues (2015), a growth mindset is not just an "attaboy" approach. Students can't succeed just by hearing that they are doing a good job; they must actually *learn* something. And vocabulary is a great "something" for students to learn because it is essential to and intertwined with everything they do at school.

CONCLUSION

We are learning more about how the brain and memory work. Understanding the brain's memory systems, as well as how the reading and language systems interact with storing vocabulary, will help you move forward with your vocabulary instruction and foster your own growth mindset about your success as a vocabulary teacher. No matter what subject you teach, there is a vocabulary that students must learn to understand concepts and procedures. When you add to that specialized vocabulary the academic words that overlap content areas and, in some cases, grade levels, our mission—upgrading our students' vocabularies—is clear. Sharing the wonders of the human brain, promoting the mindset that all brains can learn, and showing that you respect all learners' brains will help create an environment of optimism. In Chapter 2, we launch into the encoding process and explore ways to reach students with new and amazing words.

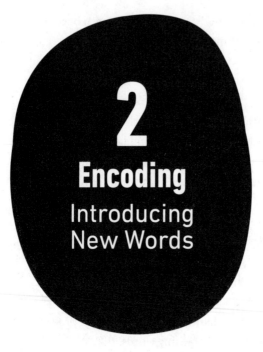

2
Encoding
Introducing New Words

It was so gratifying to have my 3rd grade grandson, Jack, come to my house after school and give an actual response to my customary question "What did you learn today?" He said, "Gram, I learned a word today. It was a word that meant something I knew about, but I didn't know there was a word for it."

I leaned in for this one. Jack continued, "Do you remember how mad Grampa got when we were at the airport for our trip to Disney? He went up to the desk at the gate to get his seat number, and the gate agent told him he didn't have a seat for him. The color of Grampa's face changed to red! He yelled, 'What do you mean you don't have a seat for me? I paid for this ticket months ago. I was told that I would be assigned a seat at the gate. Here is my ticket. You cannot bump me off this plane.' You got up to calm him down. Remember?"

"Oh, yes, Jack, I remember," I replied, wondering what all of this had to do with Jack's new word.

"Well," Jack continued, "the airline overbooked the flight! The airplane was overcrowded because they sold more tickets than they had seats. They call it *overbooking*! I've heard Mommy and Daddy say they 'booked' their flights, and I wondered what that meant. But now I know what that means and I know that sometimes airlines overbook."

Jack was so satisfied with his new word knowledge that I couldn't just let it go. So I asked, "Jack, does overbooking only happen with airplane rides?"

He answered, "You can overbook your life, too! Miss Michelle had a book on her desk called *The Dog Ate My Planner: Tales and Tips from an Overbooked Life.* Hector saw the book and read the title. That's when we started talking about the word. Everyone wanted to know what an overbooked life was. I got to tell Grampa's story, and kids started raising their hands and talking about other overbookings. Do you know when I go to the doctor's office and sometimes we have to wait an hour? That's because the doctor's office overbooked the appointments! Know what else can be overbooked? TV talk shows. They announce who's going to be on the show that day, and then sometimes they don't have time for all the guests to be on the show! See, Gramma? OVERBOOKING!"

Jack went on to describe how Miss Michelle had put the students in small groups to create skits about overbooking. His group performed a skit about an overbooked restaurant that had to turn away customers who had reservations—and boy, were those people mad!

My grandson and his classmates had had a lovely introduction to a new word. The examples were relevant and tapped into their emotional memory, so they would find it easier to remember the word. Miss Michelle had done a good job beginning the *encoding* process.

The strategies in this chapter focus on encoding. Because this is the first stage of building long-term memory, our focus is on piquing students' interest and introducing vocabulary in ways that resonate with them. An important first step is to model your own love of vocabulary. Word walls help with this. If you know the 300 Tier 2 words you want to teach during the school year, or even just the few words you're planning to introduce in an upcoming unit, let students see some of them up on bulletin boards or, my favorite, on windows. Just seeing the words "primes" the brain for learning them.

ENCODING STRATEGIES: INTRODUCTIONS THAT "REACH" KIDS

1. Put grammar in its place. One of our goals is for students to be able to put vocabulary words into sentences. Knowing which part of speech a word is will help with that process. To use this strategy, create a chart with four columns labeled *Noun, Verb, Adjective,* and *Adverb.* Go over these four parts of speech with your class; you may need to introduce them to some students. Then, when you introduce a new word, write it in the appropriate column. You may want students to keep their own POS (Parts of Speech) charts. Once a word is in the correct column, talk about the different forms of the word. For example, *"Predict* is a verb. What's the noun form? That's right: *prediction.* Is there an adjective form? *Predictable.* How about adverb? Yes, *predictably."* With this strategy, your students learn four words for the price of one!

2. Puzzles to pique curiosity. Willis (2014) suggests cultivating curiosity by cutting an image or a graphic into puzzle pieces and adding a new piece to the puzzle on the wall each day until the puzzle is complete and you are ready to present the word to your class. You could also create a puzzle with the written word cut strategically so that the final piece reveals the word. Students love guessing what the word might be as new pieces are added.

3. Wear the word. In my classrooms, I sometimes write a new word and several of its synonyms on pieces of masking tape and tape them on my body. I do not say anything about the word for some time; sparking curiosity and keeping my students engaged is key. When I think they are ready—that is, once they have looked at the words, whispered about the words, and perhaps tried to pronounce the words—I begin. Here's how I might use this approach in a K–2 classroom:

First, I ask the class, "What have you noticed that is different today? Yes, I have tape all over me! What do you see on the tape? Words. Let's take a look at the words." I take off the word we'll be learning and say, "This is a special word. It is *curious.* Repeat the word after me: *curious.* Let's try that one more time: *curious."* I put the word on the board and continue,

> Has anyone heard me use this word? You have? How did I use it? That's right! I used the word when we were talking about the story we read. I said, "I am very curious about how this story ends." Were you curious about how the story ended? What made you curious? You became curious when the young boy, Thomas, spilled his milk? I became curious then, too. Something else made me curious. Would anyone like to guess?

Students share their suggestions. Then I ask, "Well, what do you think *curious* means?" Together, we come up with a kid-friendly definition. Finally, we look at all the other words I am wearing. I take the words off one by one and have the students pronounce them after me: "I have the synonyms *interested, inquisitive, nosy,* and *prying.*"

4. Open with a cloze. A cloze exercise is a great way to introduce a new vocabulary word. It consists simply of creating sentences that leave out a key word (see Figure 2.1). Students fill in the blanks with a word or phrase based on what they understand from the surrounding text (Overturf, Montgomery, & Smith, 2013).

2.1 / Cloze Activity for Introducing Vocabulary

1. When my dog is not barking at strangers, she is usually _____.
2. The _____ smell I noticed was the rotting, wet wood.
3. The _____ waves were dangerous, but we surfed anyway.
4. The witnesses provided a _____ account of the accident.
5. If you do not wash your hands often, you may _____ the spread of the flu.
6. I love to buy shoes even though I have a _____ of them.

Answers (in order):

placid
noxious
billowing
credible
hasten
plethora

To use this strategy with your class, write a "cloze" sentence for each of the words you are about to study on the board, drawing a blank line to stand in for each vocabulary word. Read the first sentence with students following along, and have students suggest words to fill in the blank. Post all the suggestions on the board. After students have run out of ideas, read each version of the sentence (or call on students to read the different versions), inserting the suggested words one by one. After all of the suggested words have been tried, tell students what the vocabulary word is. It may or may not be one of the words that the students brainstormed. After going through all of the sentences in this manner, discuss each new vocabulary word with the class and celebrate all of the synonyms they have generated for each word.

Although this is an introductory activity, it can also be used for rehearsal or review or to test student comprehension.

5. WKWL. This is a variation of the KWL chart first developed by Donna Ogle. Start by drawing a four-column chart and labeling the columns *W*, *K*, *W*, and *L*. Beneath each letter, write what it stands for: *W* = *Word*, *K* = what we *Know* about the word, *W* = what we *Want* to know, and *L* = what we *Learned*. Now write a new vocabulary word in the first column—let's use the 4th grade math term *calculate*. Then have students brainstorm what they already know about the word. That information goes in the *K* column. When you have concluded that discussion, you may want to put students in groups of three or four to discuss what they want to know about the word *calculate*. If you have already discussed the definition during the brainstorming step, you can ask students what they would want to calculate. Finally, after a calculation lesson, lead a class discussion on what everyone has learned about the word *calculate*, and fill in the fourth column.

6. Vocabulary anchors. The idea of a vocabulary anchor has been around for a long time. A vocabulary anchor is a visual strategy that helps students make connections between concepts that are new to them and concepts that they already know (Winters, 2001). This strategy is particularly helpful for struggling readers and English language learners.

Begin by showing students a picture of a boat with an anchor in the water, and open a discussion on the purpose of an anchor. Once you have established that an anchor connects a boat to land, explain how students can use this visual to connect new vocabulary to what they already know. Have students draw a boat with an anchor, writing the new word on the boat and a similar word that they already know on the anchor. You may have to brainstorm to help them come up with a similar word. The sail should contain some kind of illustration of the new word, and students should also write similarities and differences of the two words outside the boat.

Figure 2.2 depicts an example of a vocabulary anchor for the word *metaphor*. In this case, the anchor word is *simile*, since it is usually taught first. The two words are similar in that they both compare two or more objects and are used to add color to writing, and they are different in that a metaphor does not use *like* or *as* and often uses a form of *to be*.

2.2 / Vocabulary Anchor: *Metaphor*

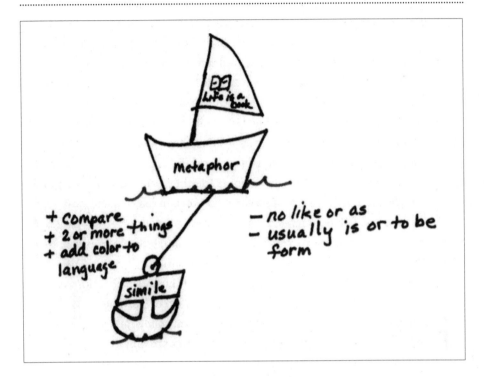

7. Vocabnotation. With today's education standards focusing on close reading and text-dependent questions, many teachers are showing students how to annotate text. Annotation simply refers to making notes while reading text. *Vocabnotation*, a word I coined, means making notes that refer to vocabulary in the text to help with comprehension. You can use various symbols or codes to represent specific notes or observations, such as

- Circling words you don't know.
- Drawing lines from words to your definition in the margin.
- "Noting" Tier 2 and Tier 3 words. ♪♪♫♪
- Drawing arrows to words that connect. ⟶

You can use this activity on new text to find out which words students don't know and decide whether to teach the words using the "fast" method or the "focused" method. Use the fast method when students have prior knowledge of a concept and you are simply attaching some new vocabulary to it. The focused method, which requires more time and more explicit teaching, is intended for more difficult words that students cannot easily connect to prior learning.

8. Graffiti graphics. This strategy, adapted from Spencer and Guillame (2009), works well to introduce new vocabulary from a text you are about to read in any subject area. Its purpose is to have students come up with their own ways to make the word more meaningful and memorable to them. Divide students into groups of four or five and give each group a different vocabulary word, along with a large piece of white paper and colorful markers. Each group writes its word in the middle of the paper. Encourage students to get creative here; for example, a group that has the word *mountain* can write the word in the shape of a mountain. Then give students 10–15 minutes to write or draw whatever they can think of to help explain the word: pictures, symbols, sentences, names, definitions, and so on. Cruise the room and help groups whose members don't understand the word at all or have a misconception about the word. When they finish, post the papers on the wall and have a spokesperson from each group present his or her group's word.

9. Miming or acting. Sometimes it's fun to walk into my classroom and begin acting out a word. The students stop whatever they are doing to watch, and it doesn't take long before they begin to try to guess the word. For instance, I might enter my 7th grade classroom talking nonstop, as fast as I can. Students shout, "Talkative!" "Chatty!" and even "Verbose!" Eventually, through consultation of their tablets, dictionaries, smartphones, or a thesaurus, they figure out that I am acting out the word *garrulous*. This simple strategy works well with students across all grade levels, as well as English language learners.

10. Let's label. According to Jensen (2013), young children label items (mostly nouns) wherever they go; these "labels" are the words from which vocabulary is grown. This labeling process tends to happen less frequently in both low-SES and nonnative-English-speaking homes. You can use the following brainstorming activity before beginning a new unit or topic as a way to level the playing field for low-SES students and English language learners.

Let's use the example of a 5th grade science lesson on earthquakes. The typical "labels" associated with this topic are *earthquake, tsunami, epicenter, fault, Richter scale,* and *magnitude.* Now follow these steps:

1. After a brief introduction to the topic, put students in small groups and have them brainstorm words related to *earthquake*: some labels they may come up with include *shake, cracks, damage, injuries, aftershock,* and *tremors.* Encourage students to come up with as many labels associated with each word as they can to further expand the word list. If you find that many students are having difficulty with this task, you can provide a list of labels for the content and discuss each one. Once students understand the words, ask them to generate labels for each.

2. Ask students to create sentences using the words they generate. For example, "There was an earthquake in California that was very high on the Richter scale."

3. Have each group team up with another group and compare their labels and sentences. By the end of a 20-minute session, most of your students should have formed numerous connections to the topic, along with mental images from the stories, movie plots, personal experiences, and other associations shared by their classmates.

4. Compile a class "master list" of labels to display on the wall or a bulletin board.

5. As you begin the unit of study, refer to the master list to help students make connections as you proceed at a deeper level.

11. Dump and clump. This activity engages students' critical thinking skills (Rogers, Ludington, & Graham, 1999). Here's how to do it:

1. Introduce the topic, and then group students into pairs or teams of three.

2. *Dump*: Each group brainstorms a list of words, items, or new information related to the topic of study.

3. *Clump*: Students categorize (clump) and label words from the "dump" word list.

4. Each group writes a descriptive summary sentence for each category, using the words in that category.

5. Upon completion, these sentences are posted around the room or shared in small groups.

The conversation that goes on in each group during this activity will help students understand and retain the words. Depending on the content and students' grade level, you may choose to provide the "clump" categories or have students create their own. Figure 2.3 provides an example of this activity.

2.3 / Dump and Clump

Directions: Brainstorm words related to your topic and place them in the "dumpster." Then pull your words out of the dumpster and clump them into categories. Finally, assign your category labels and write a summary sentence for each category.

Topic: Apps on My Smartphone

The Dumpster

Flashlight	Learn Spanish	Angry Birds	Word
Minecraft	PowerPoint	Calculator	Facebook
Instagram	Plants vs. Zombies	Twitter	Word Bingo
Math Bingo	Weather		
	Subway Surfers		

The Clumpster

Label the top of each arrow with a category name and clump the words that go into that category below.

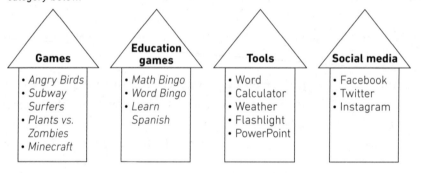

Games
- Angry Birds
- Subway Surfers
- Plants vs. Zombies
- Minecraft

Education games
- Math Bingo
- Word Bingo
- Learn Spanish

Tools
- Word
- Calculator
- Weather
- Flashlight
- PowerPoint

Social media
- Facebook
- Twitter
- Instagram

Summary Sentences

1. I have several games on my phone that keep me entertained, including *Angry Birds, Subway Surfers, Plants vs. Zombies,* and *Minecraft.*

2. *Math Bingo, Word Bingo,* and *Learn Spanish* are apps on my phone that are educational games.

3. I keep several tools on my phone to help me, such as a Word program for writing, a calculator for math, a weather app to keep me up to date on current conditions, a flashlight to help me in the dark, and PowerPoint to work on presentations.

4. Facebook, Twitter, and Instagram are apps that keep me in touch with others.

12. Word splash. This activity was developed by Dorsey Hammond of Oakland University in Rochester, Michigan. Begin by selecting key terms from a text that students will be assigned to read. Put the topic or main idea in the center of a piece of paper, and surround it with the key terms. To make it look like a "splash," write the words at funny angles, as shown in Figure 2.4. Before students read the text, have them predict, as a class or in small groups, how the terms relate to the main idea of the reading. They can create sentences predicting the relationship between the main idea and key words. Some of the sentences and phrases they come up with may be a bit crazy, but the exercise is fun and motivates students to read the text and discover how the words are used. During reading, students will check the accuracy of their sentences, and after reading, students will revise their predictions based on the text.

As a variation, have students skim a text, selecting 7–10 words or phrases, and prepare a word splash for another group to use before reading the text. Ask them to choose words that may seem contradictory to the others.

2.4 / Word Splash

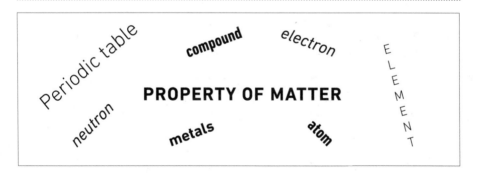

13. Out of sorts. Vocabulary sorts are used to match a vocabulary word with a definition and a picture representation or example. Follow these steps:

1. Distribute index cards that separately list vocabulary words, definitions, and pictures/examples.

2. Have students put the cards into the appropriate category (word, definition, example) and match them correctly.

3. The cards can be reused, or students can glue the cards onto a chart to keep as a study resource.

14. Affix organizer. For this visual strategy (see Figure 2.5) that teaches students about affixes, begin by drawing a rectangle on a sheet of paper, leaving an inch-wide margin on each side. In the middle of the rectangle, draw a horizontal oval. Within that oval, draw a smaller oval. If you like, you can draw lines to form four clear quadrants. Now make copies for your students or have them draw their own, individually or in pairs, and follow these steps:

1. In the inner oval, write a common affix. (Figure 2.5 uses the prefix *un.*)

2. In the outer oval, write four words that begin with the prefix, one in each quadrant.

3. In the rectangle outside the oval, write a definition for each word you have written.

4. Outside the rectangle, in each corner of the paper, write a sentence using each word.

Many students across all grade levels lack familiarity with prefixes, suffixes, and root words (Graves, 2006). See the pieces and parts strategy (p. 35) for more on this important topic.

2.5 / Affix Organizer

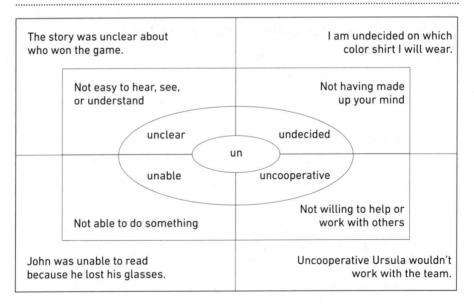

15. Related words. This strategy works well as a pre-assessment before reading a text, although it can be used as a post-reading assessment as well. Simply give students a list of 10–12 vocabulary words and have them write a few sentences that relate two or more of the words using this simple format: "I would relate _____ and _____ because . . . ."

16. Vocabulary song lyrics. This fun, creative exercise has students write expanded definitions of rich, conceptual vocabulary words in the form of a song. They can rewrite existing song lyrics or create their own. Here's an example of "Row, Row, Row Your Boat" rewritten with the word *classify*:

> Class, class, classify,
> It means to organize,
> Put it together and sort it out,
> That's how we categorize!

17. Visual strategies using technology. Enter a word in an online visual thesaurus like Visuwords, Visual Thesaurus, or Lexipedia, and watch what happens. Each of these resources provides not only a root, definitions, and examples for each word but also strategic connections to other words. Students can replace a "worn-out word" in their text with a new appropriate word of their choice. Have students reread a text several times to hear different words in use and build understanding. (As with any online tool, preview the sites and words for appropriateness.)

18. Linear arrangements. This strategy (Berne & Blachowicz, 2008; Nilsen & Nilsen, 2003) has students put words of a given category (*temperature* in the case of Figure 2.6) into a graphic continuum according to shades of meaning, much like the vocabulary paint chip strategy (described in my book *Vocab Rehab*). You can also use sticky notes and have students make colorful columns instead of the horizontal continuum. As Figure 2.6 shows, you can provide students with the first and last entries.

2.6 / Linear Arrangement

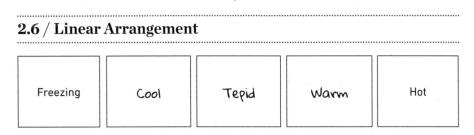

19. Enriching the vocabulary experience. This activity tests memory and builds vocabulary connections. Ask students to take out a blank sheet of paper and tell them that you are going to read aloud some words (5–20, depending on grade level) that will be included in the upcoming unit. Explain that when you say each word, you want students *not* to write down that word, but to jot down two other words or ideas that the word brings to mind. Pause for 10–20 seconds between words. When you finish, ask students to turn their papers over and try to remember the original words you said. Then let them turn their papers over again and look at what they wrote for each word you spoke. Any words that they were not able to recall should come to mind when they see the connecting words.

This activity should prime students' brains so that when they next encounter the words, they have a familiarity with them and a better comprehension of what they are reading.

20. "Pass" words. Our students are used to remembering passwords for various technologies and applications that they use. Now you're going to require them to give *you* "pass" words in certain situations. For example, before they move to a new learning station, you may ask them to give you a synonym or a definition of a word you supply, or to use it in a sentence. These "pass" words are basically the vocabulary that you are about to teach. If you are not sure your students will be able to "pass," have them work in small groups or pairs to come up with the answer.

21. Online dictionaries. A new breed of online dictionaries goes beyond the traditional, static model to provide a dynamic, engaging support for many students. For example, Lingro provides immensely helpful support for all students, especially English language learners. Go to lingro.com and type in a website that you want your students to read and understand. Now when students click on any word on the web page, a dictionary definition will pop up. Lingro can also translate words into 12 languages.

Shahi is another online dictionary—with a twist. Go to blachan.com/shahi and type in a word, and the site provides definitions and parts of speech along with illustrative images from Flickr, Google, and Yahoo. This is another great tool for English language learners.

WordHippo is yet another good resource for English language learners. Go to wordhippo.com and type in a word, and the site will provide its meaning, another word for the term, its opposite, its pronunciation, other words that rhyme with the term, and more. WordHippo will translate the word into multiple languages as well.

22. Animoto. This website (animoto.com), which allows you to make short video clips, is great for introducing new vocabulary. The site offers music, videos, and photos that are ready to use; all you need to do is decide on your theme and add some text. You can also upload your own photos. Learning a new word through an Animoto video is an impressive, engaging experience for students. You can even let students create their own videos through the site.

23. It's in the bag! Create a class vocabulary bag. Every time a new word is introduced, have a student write it down on a small piece of cardstock and put it in the bag. You will find that the more ceremonial you make this practice, the more important the word will seem to your students. The vocabulary bag provides many opportunities for rehearsal and review that we'll discuss in Chapters 3 and 4.

24. Word expert cards. This strategy (Richek & McTague, 2008), which combines direct instruction, word study in context, and peer teaching, works well when students need to learn vocabulary from a work of literature or a social studies or science text. Word expert cards can be used in 2nd grade and beyond.

Here's how it works. Before your class begins studying a new chapter or text, create a vocabulary list, including the page number where each word appears, and assign two to five different words to each student. Students are responsible for thoroughly learning these words and teaching them to their classmates.

For each word they're assigned, students prepare a card using a sheet of construction paper that includes an illustration of the word, its dictionary definition, its part of speech, the sentence from the text where it appears, and a sentence made up by the student that uses the word. Some teachers use index cards, but I find the larger the writing space, the more information I get.

Once you have approved students' cards, the peer teaching portion of the activity can begin. Working in pairs, the students take turns teaching their words, revealing the information on each card step by step and asking their partner to try and figure out the word's meaning. The "word expert" can also begin by showing his or her partner only the illustration and seeing if the partner can figure out the word. After 7–10 minutes, the students change partners. After the first day of peer teaching, you can begin the new unit or text, giving students 10 minutes each day to continue their paired vocabulary learning.

25. Word up! This strategy helps students focus on listening and makes them aware that the words being taught are important. Use the following steps (Richek & McTague, 2008):

1. Identify words from the text (e.g., novel excerpt, short story, or news article) you are about to read aloud to your class, and write them on cards.

2. Distribute one or two cards to each student.

3. Read the selection aloud. Students hold up the appropriate card each time the word is read.

26. Brain power words. Students often skip over words they don't know. This strategy (Richek & McTague, 2008) slows them down and provides time to get to "know" a word. This exercise also promotes student cooperation and interaction. Follow these steps:

1. Assign small groups of students to preview sections of a text and identify difficult words. For long chapters, assign different sections to different groups.

2. Ask students to place a sticky note next to each word that they identify as potentially difficult.

3. After finishing its section, each group goes back and uses context clues to hypothesize what the identified words might mean:

   • *Substitution*: Students can try substituting a known word that would make sense in the context.

   • *Clues of definition*: Students can look for a definition of the word in the text (this is common in textbooks, especially for Tier 3 words).

   • *Clues of opposition*: Words such as *not* and *unlike* are excellent clues to what a word is *not* and thus can help students decipher the word's meaning.

4. After students are finished identifying and defining the unfamiliar words, they check their work with their teacher.

27. Word collections. Explain to your class that just as people collect coins, stamps, model cars, and *Star Wars* figurines, this activity (Haggard, 1986) will have students "collect" two words that they believe are interesting and important enough for their classmates to learn. You may look ahead with them at upcoming topics, or they may bring in general terms. Have students write their words on the board as they enter the room. Model your appreciation of the words, assuring students that all their words are important. The class should then winnow down the list to a predetermined number of most important words by eliminating duplicates and words that most already know. The final list becomes the focus of vocabulary activities for the next few days.

28. Pieces and parts. More than 50 percent of multisyllabic words beyond the most frequently used 10,000 words contain a Greek or Latin word part. Because Greek-derived and Latinate words are so common in academic language, it makes sense to learn the highest-frequency word parts. Some studies (Graves, 2006) have shown that students in the middle grades know very few prefixes, suffixes, and roots.

What's the best way to teach these? Begin by assessing students' current knowledge of the 20 most common prefixes, shown in Figure 2.7. Graves suggests beginning with the first six prefixes and not moving on until these are mastered.

2.7 / The 20 Most Common Prefixes

Prefix	Meaning	Example
un	not	unhappy
re	again, back	return
in, im, ir, il	not	indirect
dis	not	discover
en, em	cause to	enjoy
non	not, opposite of	nonsense
in, im	in or into	inside
over	too much	overdue
mis	wrongly	mistake
sub	under, lower	subway
pre	before	prepare
inter	between, among	Internet
fore	before	foregone
de	opposite of, down	detract
trans	across	transport
super	above, beyond	Superman
semi	half	semisweet
anti	against	antiwar
mid	middle	midterm
under	too little, below	underdog

Note: You can use this chart as a pre-test by removing the meanings and examples.

I like to introduce prefixes by putting up or drawing a smiley face on the board and writing the word *happy* beneath it. Then I ask students what they would need to do to change this happy face to a sad one. I get all kinds of answers—except mine. After listening to their responses, I tell students that I can change this happy face with just two letters. Then I add "un" to *happy* and, if I am using PowerPoint or an interactive whiteboard, I can set it up beforehand so that the face changes at the push of a button. We continue the lesson by generating more words that have the same prefix, comparing definitions of those words, illustrating the words, and writing sentences using the words.

29. Vocabulary journal page. I strongly believe in vocabulary notebooks and scrapbooks. I prefer simple three-ring binders in which students can place vocabulary activities of all kinds. Students can add graphic organizers, pictures, and index cards using a hole punch or by gluing or pasting them on a sheet of paper. A vocabulary journal page is a great way to begin a discussion about a word. Figure 2.8 features a possible journal page.

2.8 / Vocabulary Journal Page

My new word is . . .	*magnetism*
It is related to . . .	science
I found it . . .	in my textbook
I think it means . . .	what magnets do
Definition	the force that pulls two magnets toward each other
Example	when my mom puts up my artwork on the refrigerator with magnets
Picture	

30. So many words, so little time. This strategy uses word-dense literature as an engaging way to teach vocabulary. One of my favorite novels to use with my literature classes is *To Kill a Mockingbird* by Harper Lee. The book is rich with vocabulary words, so I can easily pick and choose which ones to teach depending on whether I'm working with 8th graders or sophomores. Imagine going through the following passage and picking out Tier 2 or 3 words to teach:

> I mumbled that I was sorry and retired meditating upon my crime. I never deliberately learned to read, but somehow I had been wallowing illicitly in the daily papers. In the long hours of church—was it then I learned? I could not remember not being able to read hymns. Now that I was compelled to think about it, reading was something that just came to me, as learning to fasten the seat of my union suit without looking around, or achieving two bows from a snarl of shoelaces. I could not remember when the lines above Atticus's moving finger separated into words, but I had stared at them all the evenings in my memory, listening to the news of the day, Bills to Be Enacted into Laws, the diaries of Lorenzo Dow—anything Atticus happened to be reading when I crawled into his lap every night. Until I feared I would lose it, I never loved to read. One does not love breathing.
>
> I knew I had annoyed Miss Caroline, so I let well enough alone and stared out the window until recess when Jem cut me from the covey of first-graders in the schoolyard. He asked how I was getting along. I told him. (Lee, 1960, p. 4)

Before beginning each chapter, I would have students skim the pages and pick out the words they didn't know. Then they would make a chart on notebook paper listing the words and their page numbers and take a stab at the definition. I might put the students in small groups of four and have them compare lists and discuss possible definitions. If, after the discussion, they felt confident in their understanding of a word, they could put a checkmark next to it. I would then collect the papers and choose the words that I needed to cover.

31. Story impressions. Also called *semantic impressions*, this prereading strategy "arouses curiosity and allows students to anticipate what stories might be ahead" (Vacca, Vacca, & Begoray, 2005, p. 156). It can be used in different content areas. Denner, Mcginlfy, and Brown (1989) found that students who engaged in this strategy before reading a story were able to correctly answer significantly more comprehension questions after reading the story than were students who hadn't completed the prereading activity.

Here's how it works:

1. Choose key words from a story or chapter, keeping them in the order in which they appear.

2. Write the words on the board and discuss each one with the whole class. Simple definitions and descriptions will do at this point.

3. Lead the entire class in writing a story that uses the words. Students may also do this in small groups, but the first time you use this strategy, I suggest having the whole class work together. The story must have a beginning, a middle, and an end.

Students must use the words in order, but once a word is used, it may be used again. They may also use any form of a word (e.g., singular or plural; present, past, or future tense). Because students are creating a personal narrative of sorts, these words will come to life and make reading the text much more meaningful and easier to comprehend.

The story impression below was written by a student in my literature class, and the words come from Chapter 1 of the book *Pax* by Sara Pennypacker. The list of words and sentence fragments I gave students included *the fox, his boy, sniffed, woodlands, encountered, smelled green and urgent, anxiety, crying, vulnerable, grasped, scruff of the neck, wrench away, bounded, engine roared, Peter,* and *Pax.*

> A fox and his boy sniffed the air in the woodlands. They encountered lots of wildlife. The plant life they saw smelled green and urgent. When they realized they were lost, they both felt the anxiety. The boy started crying. The two were vulnerable to any wild animals or strange people they might come across. Suddenly a coyote presented himself. The fox took a fighting stance as he wanted to save his boy. But the boy grasped the fox by the scruff of his neck and had to wrench him away. The boy bounded through the woods. Finally, they heard an engine roar and ran towards the sound. They found a man in a truck who offered to take them home. The man asked the boy his name. He said, "I am Peter and this is my fox, Pax."

CONCLUSION

Have you ever heard a new word that you decided to tuck away in your brain for future use—and, a few seconds later, forgotten all about it? And it's only after time has passed and you hear the word again that you remember your intent to start using it yourself? So it goes with vocabulary. We need a strong introduction to a new word in order to create a network in the brain that is strong enough to carry over to the second memory stage: storage. The strategies in this chapter are effective, engaging ways to introduce new words and jump-start the encoding process. Chapter 3 picks up where this chapter leaves off, providing rehearsal strategies for the crucial task of putting words into long-term storage.

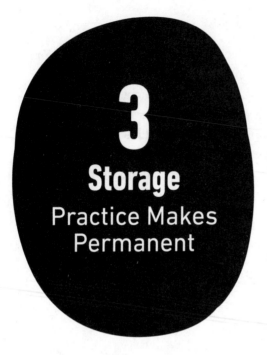

3

Storage
Practice Makes Permanent

The memory stage that comes after encoding is *storage*. To store word knowledge, students must be able to recode the word—that is, to put everything they know about the vocabulary term into their own words (both written and spoken), including a description, synonyms, antonyms, and sentences that absolutely show that they understand the term. Once students begin to use the new term in everyday speech, you will know that the word has made it into long-term storage.

Let's revisit my grandson Jack's 3rd grade classroom and see how Miss Michelle helped students put the word *overbook* into storage by leading the class through several recoding activities. First, she had students write a sentence using the word in a way that showed they understood its meaning ("I am afraid the airline will overbook my flight, and I will get bumped"). She also used the vocabulary paint chip strategy I referred to in Chapter 2 to help students understand that the word has different forms and, as an added benefit, teach them two more words. She began by distributing three-color paint chips she'd gotten from the hardware store and asked students to write *overbook* at the top of their strip. Then the students talked about the word's transformations, or the different forms this word can take. On the middle color, the students wrote the word *overbooking*, and on the bottom color, they wrote *overbooked*. They then wrote two more sentences using the transformations: "My doctor overbooked his schedule, so my appointment was late" and "This restaurant is always overbooking reservations, and we end up eating very late." The class then added these three new words to the word wall.

Another recoding strategy Miss Michelle used was the Frayer Model, a graphic organizer that students created using sheets of construction paper that they folded to make quadrants. After unfolding the paper, they labeled the quadrants and filled in the Frayer Model as shown in Figure 3.1.

3.1 / Frayer Model for *Overbook*

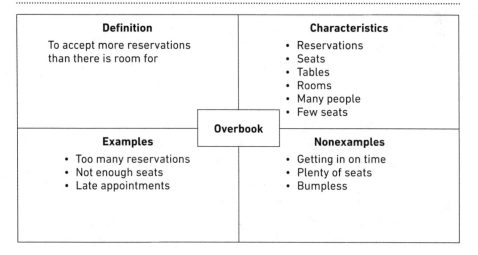

Needing to explain a vocabulary word to your students again and again is a sure sign that it's time to work on the storage stage and strengthen the weak or nonexistent network for that word. The motto of this stage is "Practice makes permanent." Once students are introduced to a new word, they will have a malleable network of neurons in their brains for the word and any related information they have learned, such as the word's definition, an image of the word, an experience they have had that connects in some way, and so on. As the word is reinforced through repetition and rehearsal, those connections get stronger. In fact, each time students use a rehearsal strategy, the network gets sturdier and builds more connections.

That's why rehearsal is the focus of the strategies in this chapter. Although some rehearsal can be rote, most rehearsal must be *elaborative* to be effective. Elaborative rehearsal, which has students think about the meaning of the term rather than simply repeat the word over and over, provides the mental "glue" that helps learning stick. Students need multiple engagements with words to form the neural networks in their brains that will lead them to full use and understanding of the word. For some students, this will take a few rehearsals, whereas other students will require many rehearsals.

There are several approaches that elaborative rehearsal strategies can take to ensure that information gets stored in long-term memory. Rehearsals can increase their power by

• *Targeting multiple memory systems.* For example, when students are using a fun, engaging strategy that integrates movement to help them remember a word, they are activating not only the procedural memory system but also their emotional memory. In addition, field trips can be a powerful strategy because the new location will trigger students' episodic memory.

• *Incorporating organization.* Organization assists memory. Graphic organizers, for example, not only provide visuals that enable students to "see" information in their minds but also help students classify and categorize new words and concepts and see how they relate to one another.

• *Funneling new words through larger ideas.* Beginning with the big picture and then filling in the details can help students make sense of new information and learn new words in context. Funneling could be as simple as writing the topic of study on the board (e.g., the Civil War) and then asking students to brainstorm words that are associated with the topic—such as *killing, slavery,* and *Lincoln*—to add to the board. As each word is contributed, the class can discuss how it connects to the topic. To introduce new vocabulary from the word list that students don't contribute on their own, the teacher can prompt the class by asking, for example, "What about *emancipation*? Where could it be connected on the board?" After some class discussion, the teacher can write it on the board near a related word (in this case, *slavery*).

• *Using synonyms, antonyms, examples, and nonexamples.* These are all excellent tools for helping students remember vocabulary words. The brain stores information through similarities but retrieves them through differences

(Feinstein, 2013). Knowing what is similar to the word being studied helps students form larger networks in the brain, and the subtle distinctions help students with both storage and retrieval. Antonyms help students isolate the meanings of words.

REHEARSAL STRATEGIES FOR LONG-TERM STORAGE

32. Rooting for words. I first saw this strategy in action during a 3rd grade science lesson. Mrs. Maloney, the teacher I was observing, had read about it in the book *What Research Has to Say About Vocabulary Instruction* (Padak, Newton, Rasinski, & Newton, 2008). Her goal was to strengthen and extend students' understanding of the term *biology* and the root words that make up the word.

First, she reminded the students of their previous discussion of the word *biology* and asked them to repeat the word after her. Then students took out their vocabulary notebooks and turned to the Frayer Model they had created when introduced to the word. Students shared their definitions of *biology*, most of them being some version of "the study of life."

Mrs. Maloney posted a large sheet of paper on her bulletin board with *bio* printed in the center and told students that she wanted them to identify as many words as they could that had the root *bio*. The way they conducted this research was up to them: they could look through books at home, talk to their parents, search the Internet, or listen closely to television programs, for example. They would write any words they discovered on the *bio* sheet, placing their initials by the word. During science time for the next two days, the students discussed the numerous words they had generated, including *biography, antibiotic, biofeedback, biochemical,* and *biopsy*. Each student who had contributed a word provided a definition, and the class discussed whether knowing the root word's meaning was helpful in understanding the word.

Mrs. Maloney wasn't done. She took a corner of that bulletin board and wrote the root word *ology*, explaining to students how interesting it was that the word *biology* consisted of two root words. She asked them to take the next 24 hours to find words that contained the root *ology*. Students added such words as *psychology, zoology, geology,* and *gynecology* and discussed these words the same way they had discussed the *bio* words.

Mrs. Maloney's students loved this lesson and the fact that they were encouraged to conduct research in their own ways. This strategy works well as a review because it offers students many possible connections to the word being studied. Beyond gaining a thorough understanding of their vocabulary word, students had learned important root words that appear in countless additional words and begun to understand how words are formed.

33. Picture this. This simple strategy harnesses the power of visual learning, discussed in Chapter 1. After you introduce a word, search the Internet for pictures that represent the word and its meaning. For example, I used this method when my class was reading *Monday with a Mad Genius* (Osborne, 2009) from the Magic Tree House series. In this story, Jack and Annie take a trip to Italy during the Renaissance and meet Leonardo da Vinci. They learn that he is more than an artist; he is also an inventor. To help my students understand what an inventor is, I found and shared with them numerous pictures of inventors—some familiar, others more obscure. Through this activity, they formed connections between their prior knowledge and their new learning.

34. Show me what you know. This visual rehearsal activity is useful for most grade levels. Simply ask students to draw a picture that illustrates their understanding of a vocabulary word. I also allow students to write on their drawings. Figure 3.2 shows a student drawing of the word *evaluate* from a 6th grade social studies unit.

3.2 / Show Me What You Know: *Evaluate*

35. Locate *locate*! This activity is a fun, effective way to rehearse Tier 2 verbs, giving students the opportunity to think about the words, their definitions, and how they are used. Students' assignment is to do whatever you write on the board. So, for "Locate *locate*!" they must find the word *locate* in their text (or another source around the room). Imagine the fun students can have with "Abbreviate *abbreviate*!" "Analyze *analyze*!" or "Clarify *clarify*!" This exercise is a good one for students to do in pairs or small groups.

36. Hear it, say it, spell it. The purpose of this rote rehearsal is to make sure that students have a given word in their *receptive vocabulary* (that is, all the words that are in their language repertoire). Simply say a word and have students repeat it and spell it. Students can either spell the word aloud or write it down. This process, which is particularly helpful for English language learners, familiarizes students with the word before you lead more elaborative rehearsals.

37. Hear it, say it, spell it, rhyme it. This elaboration on the preceding strategy adds a rhyming component, which hones students' phonemic awareness—important for students at all grade levels who struggle with sound discrimination. This strategy is great for English language learners and high-risk students.

38. Mystery words. This is a great kinesthetic activity for rehearsing multiple words that can work at all grade levels. Start by pairing students up according to whichever criteria you choose—by hair length or clothing color, for example. To begin, partner A uses his or her finger to "write" a vocabulary word on partner B's back. Partner B then has to figure out which word is being written and provide a definition. Then the partners switch roles. This is a fun game to reinforce spelling and word meaning. It also forces students to visualize the words as they feel them on their back and "see" them in their minds. Movement, fun, and multisensory learning create new connections and strengthen existing ones.

39. Synonym circles. After you have introduced several new vocabulary words, find three or four synonyms for each word. Write the words and their synonyms on index cards, using one card for each word. Hand out a card to each student and tell students to find their classmates who have the synonyms for their word and form a circle. Once they have completed this task, give each group sentences in which one of the words will fit better than the others, and have the groups pick the appropriate word for each sentence. This exercise requires students to identify the slight nuances that distinguish words from one another. To heighten the challenge, have students create their own sentences to share with the class.

40. Recode, recode, recode. Ask students to write down as much as they know about the word: its definition, its spelling, synonyms, antonyms, and ways in which it can be used. Students can do this in any format you choose—a mind map, a concept map, a Frayer Model, or a vocabulary word map, for example. Most important is that you peruse the student papers and make sure they are accurate; you do not want misinformation to go into long-term memory. This activity may also be used as a formative assessment technique to measure student word knowledge and yield feedback that helps you provide more targeted teaching.

41. You can't spell *prefix* without a prefix. The affix organizer strategy in Chapter 2 (p. 30) as well as the rooting for words strategy in this chapter (p. 43) touched on the importance of knowing prefixes, suffixes, and root words. This strategy focuses specifically on the function of a prefix. Adding a prefix to vocabulary words strengthens the brain's connections to the vocabulary and will help students retain and use the words.

Using a KWL chart is a good way to begin a lesson on prefixes. First, ask your students what they know about prefixes, and write this information in the chart's *K* column (What do you *know*?). Be sure to provide a definition of the word *prefix* if students' knowledge isn't specific enough, focusing on the word *before*. Students may offer prefixes with which they are familiar, word parts they believe are prefixes, how they use prefixes, and so on.

Next, ask students what they *want* to know about prefixes, and write their ideas as well as your own in the *W* column (What do you *want* to know?). You may need to ask some leading questions, such as "What do you think we will learn about prefixes?" or "Would you like to know the most common prefixes?" Students may respond that they want to know every prefix there is or whether all words have prefixes. Once this column is complete, teaching begins. After instruction, when students have begun to master the prefix rules and definitions, you can fill in the final *L* column (What have you *learned*?).

42. Making connections with examples. Synonyms and antonyms are easy to find, especially with the help of a thesaurus, but examples and nonexamples can be tricky. Although the Frayer Model prompts students to come up with examples and nonexamples, I find that spending time on these separately can be useful for students who struggle with the concept, especially English language learners and students who come from low-literacy homes.

As an example that works for most grade levels, I begin, "If you are not my friend, who are you?" Students often jump right to *enemy*, which is certainly a nonexample of *friend*. Then I ask, "Who else could you be?" This requires more reflection. Eventually, I begin to get answers like *brother, mother, teacher,* and so on. We have a brief discussion on whether these people with whom we have specific relationships could also be considered friends. Generally, we conclude that if we were introducing these people, we would not refer to them as "friends."

From this point, you can move on to more complex or abstract words and concepts. In social studies, the word *freedom* is a good place to start. Students are usually familiar with such typical examples as a bird being let out of a cage, so you may want to prime their brains by offering freedoms to them: "Today during library time, you may read, work on homework, or do whatever else you would like!" Then ask, "How's that an example of freedom? What other freedoms do you have?" Students may offer such examples as selecting a library book, picking out their clothing, or choosing what they want to eat for lunch. Because not all students have the same freedoms, you can have them create a graphic organizer and come up with their own examples (see Figure 3.3). You may suggest that they keep these examples on half of the map, saving space to fill in nonexamples (see the next strategy).

3.3 / Graphic Organizer for Examples of *Freedom*

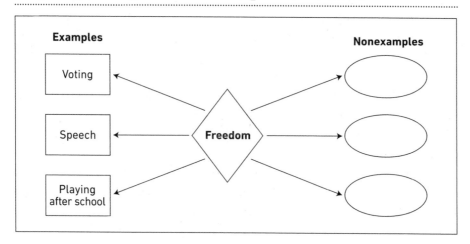

43. Making connections with nonexamples. When I taught middle school, I was forever frustrated with my students' speech. My pet peeve was their misuse of subjective and objective pronouns. The endless variations of "Jaclyn and me were on the phone . . ." were like nails on a chalkboard! The fact that I taught about sentences each year in language arts did not seem to make a difference. Students weren't forming a connection between what I was teaching and what they were saying; they were not applying the learning to their lives. I decided to do something about this disconnect. Henceforth, the nonexample became part of my toolbox. I found the following activity a great way to get students used to thinking about nonexamples for words and concepts (see Figure 3.4):

1. On the board I wrote, "The sentence: What is it?"

2. As a class, we came up with our definition: *a group of words that contains a complete thought and contains a subject and predicate in the correct matching form.* I had to push for the last part to make my point.

3. I asked students to share some of their observations from the story "The Tell-Tale Heart" by Edgar Allan Poe, which we had been reading. I wrote these on the left side of the board. (Example: "The madman thought he was smart.")

4. I asked students to share some sentences about their own lives. What a difference! I wrote these on the right side of the board, leaving some space between the two lists. (Example: "Darius and me hung out at the skate park.")

5. As we looked at all the sentences, I drew students' attention to the differences between how they wrote about text and how they wrote about personal experiences: the sentences they wrote about text were appropriate, but their personal sentences were written poorly. We checked to see whether the sentences fit our definition of *sentence*. They all had subjects and predicates, but were they correct?

6. After reading the first set of sentences, we decided that they were good examples. I wrote "Examples" above them.

7. As we read the second set, several students raised their hands to make corrections. We concluded that each of the sentences I had chosen to write on the board were not good examples, so I wrote "Nonexamples" above them. Then we corrected each sentence and wrote the revised version in the middle column.

8. The next day, we looked at our graphic organizer for examples of *freedom* (see Figure 3.3) and shared nonexamples for that word. Students came up with such words and phrases as "dependence," "being put in jail," "living under the rule of a tyrant," and "Cinderella before her fairy godmother appears."

3.4 / Using Nonexamples to Make Connections

The sentence: What is it?		
Definition: a group of words that contains a complete thought and contains a subject and predicate in the correct matching form.		
Examples	**Revised Sentences**	**Nonexamples**
• The old man's eye was weird. • The madman thought he was smart. • The storyteller went in to watch the old man sleep at midnight every night. • It took the madman an hour to put his head in the door of the bedroom.	• My mom and I went to the mall on Saturday. • Darius and I hung out at the skate park. • My brother Tony took Jacob and me to the party. • Jenny and I tried out for cheerleading.	• Me and my mom went to the mall on Saturday. • Darius and me hung out at the skate park. • My brother Tony took Jacob and I to the party. • Jenny and me tried out for cheerleading.

44. Drama queens. When introducing and rehearsing vocabulary, drama can go a long way in making connections for students, especially English language learners and struggling students who have had little or no contact with the words. Seeing you and other students dramatizing a word can leave a lasting impression.

Let's say you want to introduce the vocabulary words *exhausted* and *trudge*, which appear in a sentence of the text that the class is currently reading: "The soldiers were exhausted after trudging through the underbrush for hours." You could begin by saying, "What would that look like? Let's stand up and trudge through the underbrush!" Then model the act of walking heavily, as though you had to make your way through tangled branches, bushes, and ground cover, while saying, "It is so difficult to walk through this. I can't walk as quickly as I usually do." As students trudge with you, you can continue, "You must be exhausted. I know I am. Show me what you look like now that you are so tired." You can dramatize the word *exhausted* by placing your arm on your forehead and breathing slowly and heavily. Encourage students to imitate you and add ideas of their own, like falling down and struggling to get up.

By engaging in this activity, students have *experienced* these vocabulary words. They have seen them, heard them, and felt them—emotionally as well as physically. Students have made multiple connections to these words that will strengthen the memory of them and help place them in long-term memory.

45. Clusters. Consider teaching and rehearsing words in thematic clusters to give students the opportunity to make connections among them. Choose a group of about six words that share some common characteristics, and have students follow these steps:

1. Draw a table on a blank sheet of paper with a column for each word, plus a blank column on the left.

2. Write down a list of characteristics in the blank column that seem to relate to at least some of the words.

3. Working in pairs or small groups, discuss each characteristic in turn and whether it connects to each word. Insert a plus sign (+) for each word that has the characteristic, a minus sign (–) for each word that does not have the characteristic, and a question mark (?) if you're not sure.

4. Review the words with the rest of the class, comparing and contrasting them according to the characteristics they have or lack.

Here are some content-area examples of word clusters:

- Math: *angles, acute, right, obtuse, straight, reflex*
- Science: *cell, nucleus, mitochondrion, cell membrane, cell wall, chromosome*
- Social studies: *colony, ethnic group, migration, society, settlement, settler*

46. It's all in the bag. If you are using vocabulary bags (see p. 33), this is a great rehearsal. Follow these steps:

1. Pull several words from your vocabulary bag and write them on the board. (If your board is magnetic, you can put magnetic tape on the back of the words and stick them on the board.)

2. Divide students into pairs or small groups. I recommend small groups the first time you use this strategy.

3. Tell each group to pick a genre (e.g., fiction, nonfiction, or poetry) and then create a piece of writing in its chosen genre using the vocabulary on the board

in the order in which the words appear. You can monitor students' progress and help with language or ideas as needed.

4. Have each group divide its work in sections and designate one for each member to read. Give them time to practice their pronunciation. You can work with students on their emphasis and intonation by asking questions like "How does the character feel here? What happens to your voice when you feel this emotion? How do you want your audience to feel here? Again, how can you show this in your voice?" Model to students what you mean when necessary.

5. Ask students to read their creations aloud while their classmates listen for the vocabulary words and determine whether they are used correctly and make sense.

47. Crossword puzzles. Creating crossword puzzles challenges students to focus on word meanings; as they write clues, they must provide just enough information so that the puzzles are solvable without being too easy. After students create their puzzles, they can exchange them with peers as a class activity, or you could make copies of them for students to use at a learning station. There are several websites that allow students to create their own customized puzzles, such as http://www.puzzle-maker.com/CW and http://tools.atozteacherstuff.com/free-printable-crossword-puzzle-maker.

48. Flip-a-Chip. When Lee Mountain (2002) came up with this game, she never suspected that it would lead to improved vocabulary for so many students. Flip-a-Chip can be used at any grade level and in most content areas to prompt students to examine affixes and roots, make meaningful words, and write paragraphs using their new words. This activity is good for English language learners and students with lower levels of literacy achievement as well. To play this game, you will need poker chips—preferably white, since they will be written on—along with permanent markers, plastic bags, paper, and pencils. Here's how it works:

1. Take two poker chips. On the first chip, use a marker to print *pro* on the front and *re* on the back. On the second chip, print *duce* on the front and *voke* on the back. Begin flipping the chips and write each word you get on the board (*produce, reduce, provoke,* and *revoke*). Have a student try it, too. Keep flipping the chips until all students are convinced that they will indeed get a word with each flip.

2. Discuss the meanings of the words and the word parts. Point out how varying the pronunciation of certain words can indicate different meanings, as in emphasizing the first or second syllable of *produce*. Ask students if they have ever provoked anyone or if anyone provokes them. This allows you to discuss the different forms of the words. Make a list of other words that contain at least one of the four word parts (e.g., *invoke, induce, proclaim, reclaim*).

3. Give students a paragraph like the following one and ask them to fill in the blanks using the four original words:

> If you don't want to _____ your teacher, I suggest you _____
> the number of times you don't do your homework. In fact, the more
> work you _____, the less likely it is that she will _____ your
> privileges.

Now have students work in pairs to create their own Flip-a-Chip game. Provide each pair with four white chips, a marker, and a plastic bag. Instruct students to print four word parts on the chips, making sure that all combinations will create real words, and create their own fill-in-the-blank paragraph like the one above. Next, ask each pair to put its chips and paragraph in the plastic bag and trade it for another pair's bag. Allow time for each pair to play the game and fill in the paragraph and then meet with the pair who tried out its game to get feedback and, if necessary, rework its word choices and paragraph. You can keep the final Flip-a-Chip bags at a learning station for students to work with.

At some point, you could have students visit the ReadWriteThink website (http://www.readwritethink.org/classroom-resources/student-interactives/flip-chip-30031.html) to play Flip-a-Chip in pairs and explore different forms of words.

49. Snowstorm. In this simple activity, each student writes a word from the word wall or your current vocabulary list on a piece of scratch paper. The students then scrunch their papers up and, when given a signal, throw their "snowballs" into the air. Each student picks up a snowball that lands close by, and the class members take turns reading their word aloud and defining it. If a student's word has already been shared, he or she can offer a synonym or an antonym. The third time a word is read, the student can provide a sentence using the word or an example for the word.

50. 30-second elevator speech. Perhaps this has happened at a workshop or meeting: you get into an elevator and a student's parents join you on another floor. You realize that you have about 30 seconds to convince them that it's important for them to buy raffle tickets (or read to their child, pick their child up after school on time—anything high-priority to you). This fun rehearsal exercise has your students create their own 30-second elevator pitch to "sell" a vocabulary word. The speech must include the word's definition, how it's used, why it's important to know, and how it's superior to its synonyms. Students may present their pitches to a partner, in small groups, or to the whole class.

51. Applause, applause. This activity is a fun rehearsal of words you have been studying and offers the opportunity to use them in various ways. Begin by using a vocabulary word in the context of a sentence, and then ask students to respond in one of three ways:

1. Clap loudly if it is something that *does* apply to you.
2. Clap softly if it is something that *could possibly* apply to you.
3. Don't clap at all if it is something that *does not* apply to you.

After you model the activity, let students work in pairs to create three sentences to read to the class that should elicit a variety of responses. Here's an example of three student-generated sentences using the word *reluctant*:

- I was reluctant to change a diaper.
- I was reluctant to eat my broccoli.
- I was reluctant to go to the party.

52. What? So what? Now what? This strategy, which I have used with both students and workshop participants, provides a good rehearsal and invites students to share and hear a variety of points of view. Just ask, "What word did you learn? So what does it mean? Now in what way can you use this word in your life?" After students become accustomed to this routine, you can simply write on the board, "What? So what? Now what?" The simplicity of this strategy adds to its flexibility: for example, you can write the questions on an exit card or have students discuss the questions in small groups.

53. Vocab walk. This strategy is a variation on the gallery walk. Divide students into small groups and give each group a different vocabulary word, along with poster paper and markers. Have each group create a poster for its word, complete with an illustration, a description, synonyms, antonyms, and sentences. Put the posters up in various areas of the room and have groups move from poster to poster, writing questions or comments either on the poster or on paper you provide next to the posters. This activity allows students to rehearse their own word in depth and rehearse the other words through reflection and analysis.

54. Thumbs up or down. Write a list of five to seven vocabulary words that your class has been studying. Then write down their definitions, but scramble them so that they're separate from their respective words. Point to a word, and then point to one of the definitions. Students give the thumbs up if they believe the definition fits the word or the thumbs down if they think it's incorrect.

55. And the question is . . . This activity works especially well with nouns. Announce a vocabulary word, and have students provide the definition in the form of a question, as in the game show *Jeopardy!* For example:

> A: *Tornado.* Q: "What is a violently rotating column of air?"
>
> A: *Rhombus.* Q: "What is a shape with four equal sides?"
>
> A: *Democracy.* Q: "What is a system of government in which the people are involved in making decisions?"

56. Why should I care? This exercise has students work in pairs. Partner A says one of the vocabulary words, and partner B provides the definition. Then partner A asks, "Why should I care?" Partner B explains the word's relevance to everyday life or experience. The partners then switch roles for the next word.

57. Your number's up. Divide your class into groups of four, assigning each group a different vocabulary word, and have students number off: 1, 2, 3, 4. Give each number a different assignment: definition, synonym, antonym, sentence (you can use other assignments depending on your focus, such as example and nonexample). Then call a number and have each student with that number stand and provide the relevant information for his or her group's word. A variation of this activity is to have students find a partner from outside their group, swap information, and guess their partner's word.

58. Sell your word. Put students in pairs or small groups. Give each group one vocabulary word and have it write a commercial to "sell" its word (it's fine if students model their commercial after a real commercial). Students present their commercials to the rest of the class or even to other classes. This exercise provides an in-depth study of the word, compels students to ascertain the relevancy and value of the word, and offers an opportunity for fun and creativity.

59. Memory match. This game, which is played in groups of two to four, is based on the old card game "Concentration" (also known as "Memory"). Take index cards or colored card stock that has been cut into squares and write a vocabulary word on one card and the definition on another one. (If you wish, you can enlist students to create the cards themselves, which saves you a bit of work while giving students an additional rehearsal opportunity.) Give each pair or group a set of at least five words. You can give all groups the same set of words or give a different set of words to each group, depending on how many words the class has learned at this point in the school year. To play the game, students shuffle the cards, lay them out facedown, and take turns turning over two cards to find matches. When a student successfully matches a word with its definition, he or she gets to keep the two cards and take another turn.

60. Password, please! The classic television game show *Password* provides inspiration for this game, which has students use synonyms and examples to rehearse words. Here are the directions:

1. Have your students form pairs, and ask the partners to face each other. Give partner A and partner B each a different word list or have them each choose words from your vocabulary bag. The number of words on the list will depend on the grade level you are teaching and the number of words you want to rehearse.

2. During the first round, partner A provides one-word clues (synonyms or examples—although you may let students use antonyms or nonexamples as well if synonyms or examples are not working) about the first word on his or her list. Partner B gets one guess after each clue. Set a timer for 30 seconds (or longer, depending on the difficulty of the words). When the timer goes off, partner A records how many clues he or she had to give before partner B guessed the word. If partner B has not been able to guess, partner A records a score of 10.

3. During the second round, the partners switch roles, with partner B giving clues about the first word on his or her list.

4. The timed rounds continue until students have gone through all the words on their lists. At the end of play, partners total the number of clues given. The partner with the *lowest* score wins!

As a variation, the whole class can watch a team play the game at the front of the room, while you share the word with the rest of the class on your whiteboard. To make the activity feel even more like an immersive game show experience, you can assign a student the role of timekeeper.

61. Four-square vocabulary. Four-squares, adapted from *Word Power* (Stahl & Kapinus, 2001), are similar to the Frayer Model but a bit simpler. Here's how the strategy works:

1. Draw a rectangle on the board and divide it into four quadrants (see Figure 3.5).

2. Write "Word" in the top left quadrant, "Definition" in the bottom left quadrant, "Examples" in the top right quadrant, and "Nonexamples" in the bottom right quadrant. (The quadrant titles can be changed to suit your needs or just for variety; other useful titles include "Illustration," "Real-world uses," "Synonyms," and "Antonyms.")

3. Write the word you are rehearsing in the "Word" quadrant.

4. Have students write a definition, examples, and nonexamples of the word in the appropriate quadrants.

3.5 / Four-Square for *Freedom*

Word	Examples
Freedom	What I say, eat, read
Definition	**Nonexamples**
Condition of being free	Jail, game rules to follow, being trapped in a mine

You can have students work on this individually or in small groups. Provide time for sharing after they've completed their squares.

62. Letter categories. Divide the class into three or four teams and assign a recorder for each group. On one side of the board, write down six categories related to the current topic. For example, if the topic is weather, you might write *tornado, hurricane, thunderstorm, blizzard, lake effect,* and *flash floods.* To start the game, randomly select a letter of the alphabet and write it on the board. Each team must then work quickly to find a word for each of the six categories that starts with the chosen letter. The first team to complete all six categories shouts "Stop!" The class then stops writing, and a member of the team (someone other than the recorder) goes to the board to fill in the categories. The teacher checks each word with the class while also asking what other teams came up with for each category. If the first team has filled in each category correctly, it earns one point. The teacher then chooses a different letter, and the class plays another round.

If you have a limited amount of time, you may want to tell your students from the outset that you will be playing just a few rounds, so the team that has the most points when time runs out wins. If it will be more encouraging to your students to know how many chances they have to win, you might say, "For this game, the first team to reach 10 points wins. If we run out of time, we will continue the game during our next available time slot."

63. Connect two. This strategy, which comes from Margaret Richek (2005) of Northeastern Illinois University, challenges students to find similarities between two words. Create two columns of about 10 words each and ask students to think of something that a word in column 1 has in common with a word in column 2. Although students may initially look at the words on a superficial level, you can nudge them into deeper processing of the words by, for example, giving examples of similarities in meaning or structure. I had a student who chose the words *explain* and *describe* and said what they had in common was that they were both verbs. Our discussion of the words' meanings built on her initial observation, and she came to realize a deeper commonality between the two words: that both help people to understand and learn.

64. Two in one. This strategy, also from Margaret Richek (2005), uses the classic recoding task of writing a sentence incorporating new vocabulary words, but with the slight twist of asking students to include at least two words in one sentence. This is much more engaging and challenging for students and helps them form conceptual connections between the words. For instance, a 5th grader may write, "I am *destined* to someday become a scientist who *analyzes evidence* from crime scenes like people on the television show *CSI.*" This sentence incorporates *three* words! Richek reports that even 1st graders, with some practice, can write a sentence incorporating three vocabulary words.

65. Word treasure hunt. This review strategy takes vocabulary out of the purely academic realm and encourages students to seek out intriguing vocabulary words in their everyday environment. They may find words in any media, such as in magazines or newspapers, on television, or on the Internet, as well as words overheard in conversation or seen on signs or billboards. They then create sentences using the "treasures" they found. Take about 10 minutes twice a week for students to read their sentences to the class, and then display those sentences for a week.

This engaging exercise yields authentic examples of how words are used in different contexts and helps all students, including struggling students and English language learners, to increase their awareness and appreciation of vocabulary words.

66. A word before you leave. This activity can be a fun way to reinforce vocabulary on those days when you have just a minute or two before the bell rings. Have students think of one of the vocabulary words you have been working on and discuss the word with a partner. Then tell students that before they leave the classroom, they must give you a word and its definition. If a student's definition is incorrect, ask him or her to stand aside and listen. After a few other students have successfully given you their words and definitions, offer another chance to the waiting student, who may use one of the other students' words to leave. Making this extra effort in listening and repeating will help students with a shakier grasp on the vocabulary to solidify the information in their memories.

CONCLUSION

The night before the opening performance of a play is aptly labeled a "dress rehearsal." The stage is set for the players to perform to perfection. Yet most of us know that anything that *could* go wrong *does* go wrong at this rehearsal. Far from being a disheartening disaster, this rehearsal prepares the actors for anything: they quickly learn what they need to overcome to make opening night and every other night's performance go smoothly. Rehearsal is the means by which mistakes are remedied and performance polished. The show must go on.

So it is with memory. When words have been encoded and rehearsals have concluded, it is time for the ultimate test: can the memory be retrieved under varied circumstances? Have we provided enough opportunities, through multiple memory systems and learning modes, to ensure that our students really *get it*?

As we rehearse vocabulary with our students, we use examples and non-examples, synonyms and antonyms, drawings and drama—all of which will be stored in their memories along with the vocabulary words. We have set the stage for retrieval. This is when students will have the opportunity to access the right words across a variety of situations.

To illustrate, let's say Lakeisha's class has learned the word *devoted* and explored numerous synonyms, including *loyal, faithful, true, staunch, steadfast, constant, committed, dedicated, fond,* and *loving.* When Lakeisha writes a paragraph comparing her favorite teacher, Miss Albers, to her own mother, she wants to express the fact that her teacher is committed to her job as her mom is committed to her family, but she likes the word *devoted* more than *committed.* After giving it some thought, Lakeisha concludes that Miss Albers is *dedicated* to her profession and her students, whereas Lakeisha's mother is *devoted* to her family; in most contexts, *devoted* connotes a loving relationship that *dedicated* does not. Lakeisha's purpose in making these distinctions is not to indicate that Miss Albers isn't a loving person, but to differentiate the two women's roles in her life.

Lakeisha's knowledge of the similarities and differences between the two words helps her write and express her feelings more clearly. She is able to recall and use the correct word in any given circumstance. Chapter 4 discusses and provides strategies for retrieval: the final stage of long-term memory.

4
Retrieval
Review for Automaticity

You know how a word can just slip your mind? Even though you know it, you just can't retrieve it? When this happens, you probably substitute a synonym, which works well enough. One of the first problems people have with their memories as they age is noun retrieval, so the more synonyms you have for a given word, the less you sound like you are having memory problems. This is the purpose of the rehearsal strategies in Chapter 3: to help reinforce those neural connections and ensure that the words your students learned are in long-term memory, along with many other words connected to them.

Now the real test begins. Can students access those words? Can they speak those words correctly? Can they write using their new vocabulary? It is crucial to know that students really "know" the words. In this chapter, you are going to find out.

The third stage of memory is *retrieval*: the process by which a new word is recovered from long-term memory. This final stage strengthens the neural networks that have been formed in the brain. We know words are permanent when they can be retrieved from long-term storage, placed in working memory, and used in various situations. The downside is that misconceptions that have made it into long-term memory are difficult to dislodge, so it's important to check for understanding during the first two stages, when students are working on learning and storing new information (see Chapter 5 for more on formative assessment).

Engaging reviews help students practice and strengthen their retrieval skills. Discussion of how vocabulary words are used in various content areas and multiple contexts can also help strengthen the neural networks. Back in my grandson Jack's 3rd grade class, the students engaged in fun vocabulary games and review activities to reinforce their knowledge of the word *overbook*. For one such vocabulary review game, Miss Michelle divided the class into two teams. She placed two chairs at the front of the room with their backs to the board, and one member from each team sat in a chair. She then wrote a word (in this case, *overbook*) on the board behind the contestants. After flipping a coin to see which team would go first, she asked the first team to provide a synonym of the word. If the contestant from that team was able to name the word, his or her team got a point; if not, it was the other team's turn to provide a synonym. When the correct word was guessed, Miss Michelle asked for two more volunteers to compete, and the game continued with more vocabulary words.

Retrieval is in itself a review. Every time your students access a memory, they then re-store it. It's like taking a new route to the grocery store and then taking that same new route back; the entire trip reinforces your ability to go that way. This chapter includes numerous review strategies. *More rehearsals?* you ask. Yes. As I was told by one of my mentors, Eric Jensen, "Don't teach it till they get it right; teach it till they can't get it wrong!" An older version of this adage is "Amateurs practice till they get it right; professionals practice till they can't get it wrong." This practice is so important for your students, particularly English language learners and struggling students. Tell your students that they are no amateurs; they are "professional" speakers and writers. Not only that, but they need these "professional" words for their lives beyond school.

LOCATION, LOCATION, LOCATION

Location can be just as important for memory as it is for real estate. In Chapter 1, we discussed the fact that we can access our learning more easily in the location where we learned it—a testament to the power of episodic memory.

This factor can present a problem for students in pull-out programs. My colleague Donna used to pull students into her office for special reading instruction, but the skills she taught these kids would not always transfer to the classroom. Teachers would report that the students lacked certain abilities that Donna had seen them demonstrate in her office. I told her to try going into the classroom when her students were expected to show these proficiencies. Because we are covered with "invisible information," I surmised, Donna's presence would trigger students' episodic memories. It worked. Moreover, once students had accessed these memories in the classroom, they could continue to do so without her being there! It is important to keep this in mind when you expect your class to access their learning. Try to review and assess vocabulary knowledge in the location where they learned the words.

REVIEW STRATEGIES FOR RETRIEVAL

67. Syllapuzzles. I created this activity after playing a few word games on my phone. To use this strategy in your class, put students in small groups and follow these steps (see Figure 4.1 for an example of how it might look):

1. Choose five words you would like to review.

2. Divide the words into syllables or sections and write each word part on its own index card.

3. Give each small group a set of cards that includes all five words, along with a list of the words' definitions.

4. Have students assemble the word parts to create a word for each definition.

4.1 / Syllapuzzles

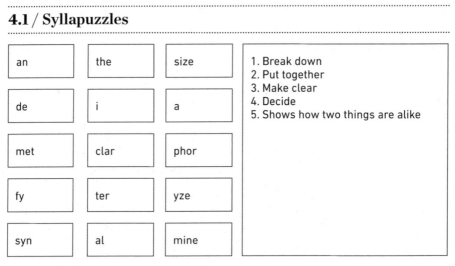

an	the	size	1. Break down
de	i	a	2. Put together
met	clar	phor	3. Make clear
fy	ter	yze	4. Decide
syn	al	mine	5. Shows how two things are alike

Answer key: 1. Analyze; 2. Synthesize; 3. Clarify; 4. Determine; 5. Metaphor

68. Walls, halls, and tossing balls. This twist on a four-corners activity, which incorporates movement and works well for students of all ages, is both an engaging way to review vocabulary knowledge and a handy formative assessment technique. Begin by determining four levels of knowledge of the vocabulary, and find a place to post a sign for each level. You can use the four corners of your room or four designated areas in the hallway, outside, or anywhere else that is available. When I led this exercise, I liked to use the cafeteria when it was free. Students must choose one of the following options and go to the appropriate location:

1. I know the word and its meaning.

2. I know the word and its meaning and can write a sentence using the word correctly.

3. I know the word, its meaning, and two synonyms and can write a sentence using the word correctly.

4. We studied that word?

A variation that can work well for English language learners is to post the words *morning*, *noon*, *afternoon*, and *night* and call out a series of activities and rituals: eating breakfast, doing homework, sleeping, and so on. Feel free to experiment and come up with your own variations, too.

Once students are in their corners, take a Koosh ball or a Hacky Sack and toss it to a student, asking the catcher to provide a definition, a sentence, or a synonym, depending on his or her level of knowledge. Then throw the ball (or ask the student to throw the ball) to the next participant.

69. Four corners with acting. This exercise works especially well if you acted out words when you first introduced them. It can be used in a variety of ways. For example, to review parts of speech, tape categories like *noun*, *verb*, *adjective*, and *adverb* to the walls or corners. Students then watch you as you act out a word, decide which part of speech it is, and move to the appropriate sign. You can also post word lists and then act out a word and have students go to the sign where the word they think you were acting out is located.

70. Back to the source. Most of the words you teach can be found in a text students are reading. For review and retrieval, going back to the source of the word can help solidify connections. To use this strategy, give students a vocabulary word they've been studying and have them follow these steps:

1. Find the word in the text.

2. Without looking at any materials, write down what the word means.

3. Talk to a neighbor, look in your vocabulary notebook, or consult any kind of authority (e.g., the teacher, the principal, or a dictionary) for the "real" definition.

4. Compare your meaning with the "real" definition.

5. Write a sentence that uses the word.

6. Determine the best way for you to remember this word—for example, by looking at the illustration in your notebook or drawing a new one, composing a song, writing a story, or recalling a memory.

71. Oh no! Students of all ages like this pronunciation practice game, which works well for small groups and is especially helpful for English language learners and struggling students. You'll need an index card for each vocabulary word you want to review, plus two additional cards. So, to review 20 vocabulary words, you'll need 22 index cards. On 20 of the cards, write a different vocabulary word; on the remaining two, write "Oh no!" Students take turns drawing a card and reading the word. If they read it automatically and easily, they keep the card. If a student draws an "Oh no!" card, he or she must return all of his or her accumulated cards to the table. Each "Oh no!" card goes out of play once it is drawn. Play until all of the cards have been drawn, at which point the student with the most cards will be declared the winner. You may want to time the game, allowing three to five minutes for play depending on the number of word cards, to add a fun level of urgency. You can also take it beyond pronunciation practice by adding more requirements to keep the card. For example, the rules could require students to recite or write down the word's definition or use it in a sentence.

72. What are you thinking? If you've ever played 20 Questions, you already know how this game goes. To make it a little easier on your students, however, you're going to include some visual clues. First, have each student pick a vocabulary word that the class is reviewing and write down 5–10 words that describe the vocabulary term. For the word *predict*, a student might write *foresee, forecast, future, envision, assume,* and *conclude.* When you call time, students must swap papers with a partner and try to figure out his or her partner's word. The first team to guess both words correctly wins.

73. Taboo words. This engaging activity provides practice in generating synonyms and descriptions. Start by dividing the class in half or into small teams of five or six. Each team must choose one member (the "guesser") to sit in front, facing the team. Then stand behind the guesser, facing the rest of the team, and hold up a piece of paper with a vocabulary word on it. The guesser's teammates then give clues for the word to the guesser, making sure not to actually say the word. The guesser will try to guess the word based on the clues. Teams have three minutes (or any amount of time you want to set) to get the guesser to say the word on the paper.

74. Scrambled words. This activity is simple yet effective, especially for English language learners. Take a list of words that your students have recently learned and write a scrambled version of each on the board. Then ask students to unscramble the words on paper. The first student to finish deciphering all the words wins. When students have finished, read the word aloud as a class. This act of manipulating the letters and trying to put them together to form words helps strengthen the network in the brain for the word.

If you have magnetic letters and a magnetic board, the whole class can engage in a fun variation on this activity. First, put up a scrambled vocabulary word and have a student come up to the board and unscramble it. Then have that student think of another word from the list and post a new scrambled word for the next student.

75. Scrambled eggs. This activity gives students the opportunity to read a high-quality, high-interest text and demonstrate their vocabulary and reading knowledge. By working collaboratively, students are able to engage in a wide range of critical thinking skills in a competitive environment.

To start, write down 10 words or phrases found in the text on strips of paper, along with the paragraph number where each can be found in the text, and put each strip into a numbered plastic egg. Set the basket of eggs at the front of the room. Then divide students into small groups and have them follow these directions:

1. Read the article individually or as a group.

2. Number the paragraphs before or while you read so that you can easily locate the vocabulary words or phrases.

3. Designate a recorder to list the numbers 1–10 on a blank sheet of paper, leaving space between the numbers.

4. Designate a runner to go to the basket and bring back an egg.

5. The runner hands the egg to another group member, who opens the egg and reads the egg number and the word or phrase that the group must define. As the group defines and discusses the word or phrase, finding evidence to support its definition in the text, the recorder writes the information by the corresponding number on the sheet.

6. The runner returns the egg to the basket and retrieves another egg. Repeat the process until the group has opened every egg and filled in numbers 1–10 on its sheet.

7. When you're done, join one or two other small groups and share your definitions.

This activity can take some time. You may use fewer words or more depending on your class's grade level or content area. Figure 4.2 shows an example of a text and two accompanying question strips.

4.2 / Scrambled Eggs: "Our Expedition"

Excerpt from "Our Expedition" by Shaun Tan

It was exciting to be on a real expedition, like venturing into a desert or jungle wilderness, only much better signposted. How great it must have been long ago, before 25 shops and freeways and fast-food outlets, when the world was still unknown. Armed with sticks, we hacked our way through slightly overgrown alleys, followed our compass along endless footpaths, scaled multilevel parking garages for a better view, and made careful notes in an exercise book. Despite starting out bright and early, however, we were nowhere near the area in question by mid-afternoon, when we had planned to be already back home on our beanbags, watching cartoons.

6. Expedition
What does this mean in the story?

7. Hacked
What does this mean in the story? Provide evidence with words or phrases that support your definition.

Students read the excerpt and respond to 10 questions or tasks related to the text's vocabulary (two of the question strips are shown here). Students discuss each word, decide on a definition, and provide the context clues that helped them understand the words.

76. Seven up. This review has students write a sentence that contains at least seven words, including a vocabulary word that you pick from your vocabulary bag or word wall. Sometimes I have all students use the same word, and sometimes they get different ones, depending on the lesson's emphasis. Each student takes turns reading his or her sentence aloud while the rest of the class (or a designated counter) counts the number of words and determines whether the sentence makes sense. You may want to do this activity in small groups the first few times. This exercise will help English language learners and others who are struggling with words. Keep in mind, though, that these words should be pretty well cemented in long-term memory by now.

77. Color my world. This creative task makes use of higher-order thinking and reasoning skills. Ask students to write a vocabulary word on a card in block or bubble letters and fill in the word with a certain color that represents that word. On the back of the card, they must explain their color choice. One of my students chose the word *future* and filled in the letters with a bright yellow. Her explanation was simple: "My future is bright!"

78. The playdough game. I love to use playdough in my teaching. I find that kids and adults alike enjoy the tactile sensation of working with playdough, and creativity abounds when they use it to sculpt a three-dimensional representation of a word or concept. This exercise activates the semantic, emotional, episodic, and procedural memory systems. You will need enough playdough to distribute to teams of four or five. I buy the small party favor–size containers so that students have some choice of color.

Ask one person from each team to come to the front of the class, and show them a flashcard with a word or phrase written on it. Then have students return to their teams and sculpt a model representing the word or phrase while their teammates try to guess it. Talking or miming is not allowed. After the team guesses the word, another member of the team goes to the front to get the next word, and the game continues. When time is up, the team that has guessed the most words correctly wins. This activity can be done with abstract concepts as well as more concrete words, but students may need to create more elaborate scenes for words such as *analyze* and *compute*.

79. Antonym bingo. This is a fun game, and helpful for English language learners and struggling students. Make bingo sheets with a 4 × 4 grid and write or paste a different word on each square. Hand out the sheets, making sure that no two cards have all the same words in the same squares, and have students mark the correct antonym for each word you call out. The first person to finish marking his or her entire page wins. Variations on this game you could try include synonym bingo and picture bingo.

I know how limited and valuable your time is, so consider recruiting students to make the bingo cards. I have had each class create a set for another class, with 1st period creating the cards for 3rd period, and so on. If you are self-contained, collaborate with your grade-level team and have classes create bingo cards for use by other teachers' classes.

80. *Indisputable* or *irrefutable*? Finding the nuances in word meanings is an important skill. As Mark Twain (1999) said, "The difference between the *almost right* word and the *right* word is really a large matter. 'Tis the difference between the lightning bug and the lightning."

Accordingly, this is a great activity to foster higher-level thinking and deep processing of vocabulary. First, write the strategy's name on the board and ask students to explore the distinctions between the two words by conducting Internet research, looking up the words in dictionaries, and consulting experts such as the librarian, teachers, and other adults. When students examine words more closely, they begin to see that there can be significant differences even among synonyms. *Indisputable* does not allow for dispute; therefore, it is true. In contrast, *irrefutable* cannot be disproved but can be questioned. After this opening exercise, have students look at their vocabulary words in their vocabulary notebooks or scrapbooks and their accompanying synonyms. Which are more or less interchangeable? Which are different enough that substituting one for the other changes a sentence's meaning? Have students discuss these questions in small groups and then as a class.

81. Tune in. Talk more. Take turns. It's time to replace the "kid language" in our classrooms with rich vocabulary. Challenge colleagues and students alike to "upgrade" their speaking vocabulary. Tune in to conversations and see if you can contribute using higher-level vocabulary. Talk to your students as though they are adults, and ask them to do the same. Take turns role-playing conversations with people whom they would want to impress. For instance, if they invited Albert Einstein over for dinner, how would the conversation go? The president of the United States? The principal? Ask students to think about which of their vocabulary words might apply in these conversations. Academic words are very useful in real-world encounters like college or job interviews, academic conferences, or professional events.

82. The sky is the limit! Are you the "lucky" teacher who got the classroom with no bulletin boards, hardly any wall space, or a wall of windows whose blinds must always be closed because they look directly into the library? I have long encouraged creating window walls as well as word walls, but even that solution won't work for everyone. I once had a colleague who could use only the floor or the ceiling as her bulletin board or "wall." The floor was a great place to set a "Welcome to Today's Word" mat but otherwise had limited possibilities. However, the teacher embraced the ceiling with the idea that "the sky is the limit," encouraging students who found new words to share them, write them on paper, and then either stick them onto the ceiling or suspend them from the ceiling on string.

83. Cloudy or clear? This activity is a great formative assessment technique and provides a helpful review for struggling students who feel too embarrassed to openly participate. Here's how it works: the teacher announces a vocabulary word, and each student holds up an index card that has "cloudy" written on one side and "clear" on the other. The teacher may call on any student who is holding up the "clear" side of the card to provide the word's definition, a sentence using the word, an example, a synonym, or some other demonstration of knowledge. Students who hold up the "cloudy" side are exempt from questioning, but they may turn over their cards to "clear" at any point if they feel comfortable contributing. At the end of the lesson, the remaining "cloudy" students must "clear things up" by working on the word in their vocabulary notebooks, filling out a graphic organizer for the word, or working with a small group of "clear" students on the word.

After listening to their peers provide word information, many "cloudy" students will feel much more confident participating. If they repeat exactly what another student has previously said, you can simply ask for different information to ensure that the student really has made the connections. Repetition alone, however, is still a great working memory practice. If a student can repeat what another student said, that means he or she has held that information in mind for a short period and, by repeating it, can get it into long-term memory!

84. The relay game. You will almost never see my students in rows, but for this review, students must have privacy to work. I like this strategy because students work together, and if there are a lot of corrections on the papers, I know which words the class needs to rehearse more. Here's how to play:

1. Divide the class into groups of four or five and ask them to line up their desks or seats in a row, one behind the other.

2. Give the first person in each row a handout on which you have written at least 10 sentences that need to be clozed or that include an incorrectly used word. If you're using cloze sentences, you can provide a list of words on the paper or have students fill in the blanks themselves with the word that they think will fit best.

3. The first student in each row must complete the first sentence and then pass the paper to the person behind him or her.

4. The second student completes the second sentence and can also check the first student's work for errors before passing the paper back to the third team member.

The first team to finish with all sentences correct wins.

85. Vocabulary association triangles. The goal of this strategy (Silver, Dewing, & Perini, 2012) is to help students create associations between vocabulary words and use vocabulary words in context. Deliver the following directions to students:

1. Draw a triangle on your paper.

2. At each angle, record a vocabulary word from the list of 20 words provided. Begin with the first three words and progress in numerical order as you create more triangles. *Advanced:* Complete the final triangle by adding word 1 to words 19 and 20.

3. After you have created your triangle, begin the word association exercise:
   a. Consider the word at each corner of the base of the triangle. You may wish to record the definition of each word next to it as a reminder of its meaning.
   b. Think about how these two words may be associated. Focus on word meaning.
   c. Along the triangle base, write a coherent sentence using the two words.
   d. Repeat steps a–c for the word pairs on the remaining two sides of the triangle.
   e. Now try to write a sentence using all three words in the middle of the triangle.

Figure 4.3 provides an example of a vocabulary association triangle for *generosity, peculiar*, and *fragile*.

4.3 / Example of a Vocabulary Association Triangle

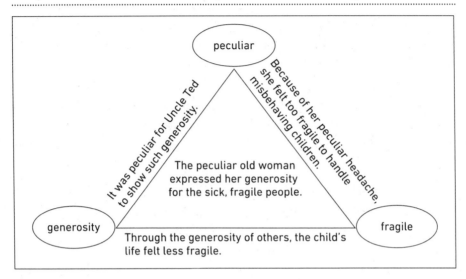

86. I write; you write. Select four to six important words and embed each in a coherent and contextualized sentence followed by a semicolon. Italicize or underline the vocabulary word. Ask students to add another sentence after the semicolon that clearly demonstrates their understanding of the italicized word as it is used in this context. For example, "Jamal felt the dog *nuzzling* against him; he liked cuddling with the animal." See Figure 4.4 for more examples.

4.4 / Examples of I Write; You Write

1. Jenny was able to *achieve* the highest Girl Scout honor; she always worked hard to be successful.

2. He is the best *candidate* for the job; he has won many elections.

3. Jack didn't know he was *endangered*; there were more wild animals in the forest than he had expected.

4. Frostbite can occur when it is very *frigid*; cold temperatures can be dangerous if you are not dressed appropriately.

5. I will *oppose* the new school hours; I have always been against longer school days.

87. Justify. Present four to six sentences, each containing an italicized or underlined word from the study list, and ask students to decide whether each word makes sense in this context. If yes, the student must justify why the sentence makes sense. If no, the student must explain why it is illogical and revise the part of the sentence that doesn't make sense.

88. Hangman. Many students are familiar with this old favorite, but some English language learners or students with poor literacy skills may not be. It makes for a fun vocabulary review. Proceed according to the following steps, substituting words and details as needed (the example here is for the vocabulary word *crater* from a unit on the moon):

1. On a whiteboard or chart paper, draw a "gallows" and a series of spaces below it representing each letter of the target word.

2. Say, "I'm thinking of a word on our academic word wall that has six letters and has something to do with astronomy."

3. Students guess one letter at a time. As each correct letter is guessed, write the letter in the corresponding blank. For each incorrect guess, draw one part of a stick figure in this order: head, torso, left arm, right arm, left leg, right leg. When you've drawn a complete body, the man is "hanged," and you can supply the correct answer. When students guess the word before the figure is hanged, move on to the next word.

89. Word wall rhymes. To play this game, recommended by Cunningham (1999), provide a clue containing a word that rhymes with one of the words on your word wall. Students must decide which word rhymes and write it down. So, for example, a 4th grade social studies teacher might ask his students to number their papers from 1 to 5, and proceed to deliver a series of clues: "Number 1 begins with *H* and rhymes with *mystery*." Students write down *history*. "Number 2 begins with *R* and rhymes with *legions*." Students write down *regions*. "Number 3 begins with *T* and rhymes with *axes*." Students write down *taxes*. And so on. After he's done reading the clues, the teacher checks students' answers by reading out the correct answers. Students then share the words they wrote.

90. Sparkle. This game is a variation on the popular spelling game and is fantastic for reinforcing vocabulary. It can be as quick as you want it to be, depending on how many words you want to review. Here's how it works:

1. The class forms a circle.
2. The teacher reads a word from the vocabulary list.
3. The first student gives the definition.
4. The next student gives a synonym.
5. The next student provides a sentence.
6. The teacher reads another word, and the game continues.
7. After the class has gone through the full cycle for three words, the next student says "Sparkle!" and is out, and returns to his or her seat.
8. The game continues, with a student saying "Sparkle!" and returning to his or her seat after every three rounds. In addition, any time a student gives a wrong answer, he or she is out.
9. The last student standing wins.

91. Who needs a wheel? This activity, inspired by the popular game show *Wheel of Fortune*, is a fun way to review vocabulary words. To prepare,

1. Decide which words you want to review, and write each word on a cue card.
2. Stick the cards facedown on the board, bulletin board, or chart paper.
3. Draw blank lines next to each card to represent the letters of the word.
4. Write out the letters of the alphabet on the chart paper or board in order to keep track of student guesses.

To play,

1. Introduce the game to students by explaining that they will take turns guessing the letters contained in each vocabulary word; if a student guesses a letter correctly, he or she can attempt to guess the word.
2. When a student guesses a letter that is in the word, write it on the appropriate blank space(s), and encourage the student to guess the whole word. Award two points if the student guesses the word correctly, and one point if the guess is incorrect but could fit.
3. When a student guesses a letter that isn't in the word, cross out the letter in the alphabet.
4. Continue until all of the words have been revealed. The student with the most points wins.
5. Now review all the words, including their meanings.

92. Dry erase formative assessment. Even in today's high-tech world, students like to write on boards. With this strategy, you can conduct quick assessments while students enjoy and focus on their task. Simply announce a vocabulary word and give a task related to it, such as "Definition," "Synonym," "Example," or "Seven up sentence," and cruise the room to observe what students write on their dry erase boards. With a class roster in your hand as you walk around, you can put a check mark next to the name of each student who completes the assigned task correctly, or you can use a simple 3-2-1 system (3 = exemplary, 2 = satisfactory, 1 = unsatisfactory or incomplete). If you already know that your students have a command of the words, you can time them or simply say "Go!" and see who finishes first.

93. Grudge ball. This is a fun review game for students of all ages. You will need a basketball hoop and a ball for students to shoot (Nerf balls work well). Follow these steps:

1. Divide students into four to six teams, depending on how fast you want the game to go.

2. On the board, draw a chart that lists each team, along with a row of 10 Xs for each.

3. Ask a member of the first team a question related to a vocabulary word. (Make sure that the teams alternate who answers the questions each time.)

4a. If the team gets it right, it can erase two Xs from the other teams, taking one X from each of two teams or taking both from one team. No suicide (i.e., a team can't erase its own Xs)! The team also gets a chance to shoot the ball. If it makes the shot, it can erase an additional X from another team.

4b. If the answering team member doesn't know the answer, he or she can ask his or her teammates. However, if the team collectively answers correctly, it can erase only one X from another team, and it can't make a shot for an extra point. This option supports students who feel too much pressure answering a question on their own.

5. The game proceeds, with each team taking turns answering the vocabulary questions.

6. When a team's Xs have been eliminated, it is still in the game and goes through the rotation. To get back on the board, however, the team must answer the question correctly *and* make the basket. If it misses, it has to wait to try again the next turn.

You can also play this game completely with teams rather than individual students answering the vocabulary question. No one is on the spot, and everyone is totally engaged. As an additional accommodation, you can draw two "free throw" lines, making the closer one worth 2 points and the farther one worth 3 points.

94. M&M game. This game, which requires a supply of M&M's, provides review with a sweet ending. Here's how to play:

1. Place students in pairs or small groups, and give each student a handful of M&M's.

2. Write six different vocabulary words on the board, assigning each word a different M&M color.

3. Students must provide a definition, sentence, synonym, antonym, or example for each M&M that they have corresponding to a word on the board.

Students may not eat an M&M until they have provided the sentence or definition for it, and they may not refuse to take M&M's.

95. To be or not to be? This collaborative peer conferencing exercise prompts students to use stronger verbs and more diverse sentence structures. Before students swap written drafts of papers with their partners to be edited or reviewed, have them circle every instance of the verb "to be" in their own drafts. This could take the form of any conjugation: *is, am, are, was, were, being*, and so on. When students' review their partners' drafts, have them, in addition to the normal peer feedback requirements, suggest how their partners could rework the sentences to eliminate the use of "to be"—for example, by combining sentences or swapping out a stronger verb for "to be." Here's an example:

> *Original:* The movie is great.

> *Improved:* The movie provided great entertainment.

96. Sentence, please. This review activity, which hones students' recall, is also an excellent assessment technique. Just give students the definition of a word and ask them to create a sentence that includes the vocabulary word that fits that definition. For example, for the word *abandon*, you could say, "Give me a sentence that contains the word meaning 'to stop caring and leave, or to relinquish.'" Students must then write a sentence using the word, such as "I felt like my mom was going to *abandon* me when she talked about moving to Colorado." If a student writes a sentence using a synonym instead, such as "I felt like my mom was going to *desert* me when she talked about moving to Colorado," ask for a synonym for *desert* that is on the vocabulary list.

97. Kick me! The first rule of this game is that there is no actual kicking! Once you make that clear, follow these steps:

1. Print vocabulary words on small sticky notes or stickers and put one on each student's back, so that students can't see their own words. Remind students not to divulge others' words to them.

2. Tell students to pair up with a classmate and begin asking qualifying questions to guess the word on their back. Questions such as "Am I a verb?" "Am I on the word wall?" "Am I a word used on assessments?" and "Do I mean *exciting*?" may guide a student to his or her word.

3. Once students have correctly guessed the terms on their own backs, they may return to their seats.

As an optional additional step, after all students have identified their words, you can have them identify the person whose word would best be associated with the word they have been given. So, for example, students would roam the room to find a synonym or an antonym or perhaps form a group with classmates whose words all fit a central theme.

98. Which sounds better? It is so important that our students learn to use Tier 2 words both in everyday conversations and in writing. I have always taught my students how to talk to people to build rapport—especially their parents, since they are often asking them for things and are eager to increase the odds of getting their wishes granted.

For this exercise, students record some of their typical conversations with a parent or other caregiver. We then take their statements or questions and make them better—that is, more specific and articulate. This activity is fun and can become competitive, in a good way, in the classroom. After students have revised a sentence, have them discuss why the new sentence is "better." Here are some before-and-after examples:

• The test was hard. *Better:* The examination included complex, challenging tasks.

• Science experiments freak me out. *Better:* Science experiments cause me great anxiety.

• I hate doing homework. *Better:* Completing work at home for class is distasteful to me.

• The school dance was awesome. *Better*: The school dance gave me great pleasure.

99. Body sculpting. For this activity, pair up students and designate one the sculptor and one the clay. The sculptor molds the "clay" into something that represents a vocabulary word, or he or she strikes a pose that the clay must mirror. The sculptor and clay switch roles with subsequent words. Although representations may be concrete or abstract, this activity works particularly well for words associated with feelings. As a variation, students can express the words in some other way, such as through dance.

100. Q&A. The ability to use a vocabulary word in a question requires a deeper knowledge of the word than does plugging it into a simple sentence. This strategy (Koprowski, 2006) also requires students to understand the word in question format and answer the question using the vocabulary word.

To use the strategy, start by writing two separate word lists on the board: an A list and a B list. Assign half the class the A list and the other half the B list. Each student takes each word from his or her list and uses it in a logical question, underlining the list word. The question should demonstrate some understanding of the word (e.g., "How did you feel when the judge granted clemency to the person who killed the mayor?" rather than "What does clemency mean?"). When the students have finished writing their questions, ask A and B students to pair up and exchange their lists of questions. The students must read each question and write an answer in which they must use the same word that is underlined in the question. After everyone has finished, partners exchange their papers again and read their Q&As. Here's an example of a Q&A:

> What qualities would you expect to see in an entrepreneur?
>
> I would expect an entrepreneur to be able to motivate people, to have good business sense, and to be hard working.

101. Cinquain vocab. A cinquain is a five-line stanza based on the Japanese haiku. Here's what a vocabulary cinquain consists of:

Line 1: A word for the subject of the poem.
Line 2: Two words that describe the subject.
Line 3: Three *ing* verbs related to the subject.
Line 4: A phrase that tells more about the word.
Line 5: The subject word again (or another word for it).

And here's an example:

Adversary

Enemy, formidable

Challenging, competing, attacking

A worthy opponent

Rival

Because this form focuses on one word, it serves well as a review strategy. If a student can provide all the components of this short poem without needing assistance, you can feel sure that he or she knows the word. Once students become comfortable with this format, you can use it as an assessment technique.

CONCLUSION

Retrieval is a critical component of our students' vocabulary knowledge. Vocabulary review strategies abound, but I hope that those in this chapter provide enough variety that you don't need to spend too much of your valuable time searching for them.

Retrieval strategies are more than just review activities; they enable the brain to access information from multiple memory systems, put all that information together, and re-store it for future use. The more often a memory is recalled, the easier it becomes to access. Games work well as retrieval activities, as the fun and mild competition engages students. Tobias, a former student of mine who came from a low-SES neighborhood and lived in a low-literacy home, approached me after a review game and said, "Mrs. Sprenger, I didn't even know I knew what those words meant, and now I know them even better!" Music to my ears.

In the next and final chapter, we'll delve into planning vocabulary lessons, assessment (pre-, post-, and formative), and possible vocabulary rubrics. Taking time to reflect on a vocabulary plan and assessment strategies that will meet your students' needs will help you determine how vocabulary can fit into your weekly lesson plans.

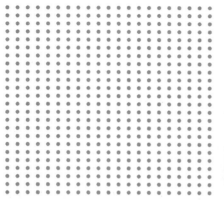

5
What Now?
Assessment and Planning

Our ultimate goal is to increase and enrich our students' word knowledge so systematically that their extensive vocabularies will be easily recognized in their speaking, writing, and reading comprehension across content areas and settings. Planning is essential to reaching this goal. Once you have created and executed a blueprint for effective vocabulary instruction, the tone of your classroom will change: word prominence and word dominance will become clear priorities, seamlessly integrated into learning and teaching.

We know that some students don't transfer memories as easily as others do, including English language learners and struggling students. As we know from previous chapters' discussion about episodic memory, even if students learn vocabulary well in our classrooms, they may have a difficult time retrieving their knowledge in other contexts. Memories do eventually get consolidated in such a way that they can be accessed anywhere. Until that happens—and it can take anywhere from two months to two years—assessing our students in the classroom is essential.

Assessment and planning go hand in hand as two critical, intersecting supports of a robust vocabulary program. This chapter addresses both.

ASSESSMENT

According to Allen (1999), assessment of students' vocabulary development should be varied and meaningful and look for several indicators of word growth, including

- An increased sense of wordplay.
- An improved awareness of how words sound (rhyme, repetitive language patterns).
- An inquisitiveness about word meanings and etymologies.
- The use of richer and more diverse language in speech and writing.

Your understanding of students' vocabulary development should primarily be drawn from formative assessment data that you collect throughout the year. One or two assessments will not cut it; you need many more data to drive your instruction. It will be valuable for students to assess their own progress as well.

Make sure to use multiple forms of brain-compatible assessments. Many of the strategies in Chapters 2–4 can be used as formative assessment techniques. Keep in mind that if you mostly use fun activities to engage your students, a traditional test may be a difficult transfer. If these assessments are part of your plan, be sure to use some quizzes or homework that are in a similar format, so students won't be blindsided when it's time for the test. The following sections address pre- and post-assessment, formative assessment, and self-assessment (for both you and your students).

Assess Yourself!

Before we delve into assessment strategies for students, take some time to fill out, either on paper or in your head, a Frayer Model examining your vocabulary instruction (see Figure 5.1). This process should help you recall strategies that worked for you, along with those that did not. Be honest! I recommend engaging in this reflection with your colleagues at some point, since professional conversation often triggers memories of standout lessons and elicits insights that may not come up during solitary reflection. The teacher who completed the Frayer in Figure 5.1 realized that she had not been making vocabulary a priority. Instead of teaching vocabulary, she had been merely assigning it. This simple self-assessment exercise showed her how important and powerful vocabulary notebooks can be and that her ELLs needed assistance with some assignments.

5.1 / Frayer Model: Reflection on Vocabulary Instruction

My current vocabulary habits (When do I teach? How do I teach? How often?)	Facts/characteristics (What strategies do I use?)
• I often assign 10–20 words per week. • I have my students look up words in the dictionary. • I expect them to write the information in their notebooks, but I usually don't have time to look at the notebooks.	• I expect my students to learn most vocabulary from reading. • I ask my students if they know a word, and when everyone nods yes, I move on. • I don't have time to teach much vocabulary.

Vocabulary Instruction

Examples (my best vocab lesson ever!)	Nonexamples (the time my vocab lesson blew up in my face!)
My best vocabulary lesson was when I put my students in groups and gave each group one word to become an expert on. They looked up the word, talked about it, and then split up to meet with one person from each of the other groups. So each student explained his or her own word. The kids loved it!	This was the worst: I handed out 20 words and dictionaries to my students. I had several ELL students in my class, and they ended up having to look up the words used in the definitions for the vocab words! I didn't realize this until the class was half over.

Pre- and Post-Assessment

The purpose of pre-assessment is to discover the information in students' long-term memories that relates to the content about to be studied. I like to use exit cards as an informal pre-assessment. Catching students before they leave class with a "ticket to leave" prompts them to use their memories to provide information. Vocabulary exit cards can be as simple as "How would you use the word *putrid* in a sentence?" "Have you ever used the word *malevolent*? How?" or "Give a word that means the same thing as *appraise*." Collect the cards before students leave. It takes little time to sort these cards into three categories: knows it, knows a little, or doesn't have a clue. If all students know a word, review it during your next vocabulary lesson and move on to others, being sure to continue using the word in class to strengthen students' memory of it. If most students know the word but some don't have a firm grasp of it, it's time to group students and differentiate instruction. The students who know the word can work on generating examples and nonexamples or writing sentences while you use encoding strategies with those who still need to gain a basic understanding. This simple practice can be very useful in helping you determine how much time to spend on different words.

Admit cards, which students fill out as soon as they enter the room, are the beginning-of-class equivalent to exit cards. These are useful for telling you how strong students' memory networks are from the previous day's learning, which is also helpful in assessing your teaching. If students don't recall much, you may need to ask yourself whether your lessons were effective. You also need to ask students if they are sleeping enough: memories are encoded while we sleep.

First word/last word is another technique that can be used for pre- and post-assessment of students' understanding of a topic. Choose a vocabulary word from the content (e.g., *discourse*) and ask students to write the word vertically on a sheet of paper, acrostic-style. Students must then use each letter in the word as the first letter of a word that is characteristic of the vocabulary word. Here's a completed first word/last word for *discourse*:

> *D* = Discussion
>
> *I* = Interesting
>
> *S* = Serious
>
> *C* = Conversation
>
> *O* = Oration
>
> *U* = Utterance
>
> *R* = Rhetoric
>
> *S* = Speech
>
> *E* = Exposition

As a post-assessment, ask students to repeat the process and then to compare their *first* word with their *last* word (Keeley, 2016).

There are numerous other possibilities for informal pre-assessment. An easy way to pre-assess is to hand out sheets on which students must circle the correct item—whether from a group of pictures or a list of words, definitions, synonyms, or antonyms. For example, you could ask students to

- Read or listen to the word and circle a picture of it.
- Look at a picture and circle the word for it.
- Read or listen to the word and write a definition.
- Read or listen to the word and circle a definition, a synonym, or an antonym.
- Read or listen to the word in context and circle a definition, a synonym, or an antonym.
- Read a sentence with one missing word (i.e., a cloze sentence) and write in the missing word.
- Listen to a cloze sentence and say the missing word aloud.
- Read or listen to the word and either illustrate it or provide a spoken description of it.
- Read or listen to the word and put it in a category provided by the teacher.
- Find the word listed under a category in which it doesn't belong.

As you can see, you can quite easily get in the habit of administering these quick (even fun!) pre- and post-assessments, which yield useful information for not a lot of effort.

Formative Assessment

As vocabulary expert and advocate Michael Clay Thompson (2009) says, "Students who don't know many words can't write many words." While students are encoding, storing, and retrieving new words, they also need to be using those words in conversation and writing and be able to recognize and comprehend these words when they encounter them in a text.

Assessment of vocabulary learning can take several forms. I believe strongly in the "show me what you know" philosophy. If a student really "owns" a word, it should also show up in his or her writing.

In addition, there are many graphic organizers that are useful for introducing, rehearsing, and reviewing vocabulary. Why not use those same tools for formative assessment purposes? For example, Venn diagrams and the Frayer Model help students organize their thinking *and* show you what they know.

With a Venn diagram, as shown in Figure 5.2, students can compare and contrast two words from their vocabulary list. If you are using a vocabulary bag, you can pull two words from it and ask students, working independently, to create a Venn diagram comparing those words. Figure 5.3 shows an example of a rubric

5.2 / Venn Diagram for Assessment: *Compare* and *Contrast*

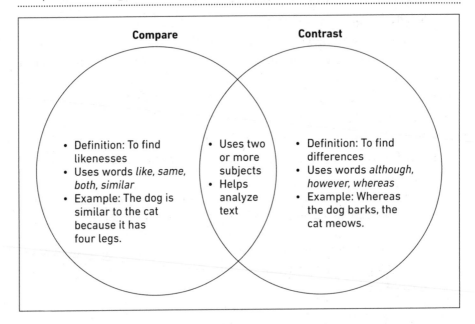

Compare   **Contrast**

- Definition: To find likenesses
- Uses words *like, same, both, similar*
- Example: The dog is similar to the cat because it has four legs.

- Uses two or more subjects
- Helps analyze text

- Definition: To find differences
- Uses words *although, however, whereas*
- Example: Whereas the dog barks, the cat meows.

5.3 / Venn Diagram Rubric

Criteria	By George, You've Got It!	Getting Close	Not Quite There Yet
Evidence	All statements are supported by the readings.	Most statements are supported by the readings.	Few or none of the statements are supported by the readings.
Placement	All statements for differences are in the outside circles. All statements for similarities are placed in the center circle portion.	Most statements for similarities and differences are in their proper places.	Few or none of the statements are in their proper places.
Number of statements	Each circle contains four comparison statements.	Each circle contains three comparison statements.	Each circle contains two or fewer comparison statements.

assessing students' Venn diagrams; I recommend customizing your rubric to fit the content rather than using a generic template, but this can help you get started.

Students can use a Frayer Model set up similarly to the ones shown in Figures 3.1 and 5.1, with the top quadrants usually labeled "Definition/Description" and "Facts/Characteristics" and the bottom quadrants labeled "Examples" and "Nonexamples." Now look at the Frayer Model rubric in Figure 5.4. Depending

5.4 / Frayer Model Rubric

Criteria	3	2	1
Vocabulary word	The word is present and contains no spelling errors.	A word is present but contains at least one spelling error.	No word is present.
Definition/ description	Clearly and fully communicates the meaning or concept of the word.	Partially communicates the meaning or concept of the word.	Does not communicate the meaning or concept of the word.
Facts/ characteristics	There are at least three facts/characteristics listed, and they accurately describe the word.	There are at least two facts/characteristics listed, but they do not fully describe the word.	There are no facts/characteristics listed; there are facts/characteristics listed, but they fail to describe the word; or the facts/characteristics are in the wrong box.
Examples	There are at least three examples listed that accurately represent the word.	There is at least one example listed, but it does not fully represent the word.	There is no example listed; there is an example, but it fails to represent the word; or the example is in the wrong box.
Nonexamples	There are at least three nonexamples listed that accurately represent the word.	There is at least one nonexample listed, but it does not fully represent the word.	There is no nonexample listed; there is a nonexample, but it fails to represent the word; or the nonexample is in the wrong box.
Illustration	Provides an illustration that clearly and fully reflects understanding of the word or concept.	Provides an illustration that reflects partial understanding of the word or concept.	Does not provide an illustration that reflects understanding of the word or concept.

on how you planned your vocabulary strategies, you may want to change the labels of some of the quadrants. For instance, if you used illustrations as a learning or review tool, you may want to have students draw a picture as part of their demonstration of knowledge. You can modify the rubric in Figure 5.4 for your own Frayer, or you can use it for a different type of assessment that requires similar information. Again, it's helpful to align teaching strategies, assessments, and rubrics as much as possible.

Finally, the cloze procedure is also frequently used for formative assessment purposes. You will probably have a word bank that your students can use to pick the word that goes in the sentence. It makes no difference if you have used cloze sentences for encoding, storing, or retrieving words; each cloze is different and new to your students. See Figure 5.5 for an example of a cloze assessment.

5.5 / Cloze Assessment

Fill in the blanks with words from the word bank at the bottom of this page.

Jerry _____ added the flour to his cookie dough. In the past, he had _____ to make the perfect cookie. He had even _____ the recipe his mom gave him, which was a recipe she _____. This time he _____ a better outcome. The plan he _____ was simple. He would mix the cookie dough _____, and then he would form the cookies _____. Poor Jerry did not know that his oven was working _____, and that made the cookies burn _____!

Word Bank

anticipated	gradually	masterfully
cherished	horribly	repeatedly
devised	imitated	struggled
flawlessly		

Student Self-Assessment

Making your students more aware of the vocabulary they use will go a long way toward increasing the number of words they know and use. At one of the many reading conferences I attended, I fell in love with a vocabulary rubric some teachers were using. What stuck with me were the colorful headings for the chart:

"Heard It!" "Said It!" "Wrote It!" and "Read It!" Inspired, I created a similar self-assessment rubric for students. In the first column, students write the word; in the second through fifth columns, students enter checkmarks to log their different types of encounters with the word. In the "Explanation" column, students explain when and how they used the word. The genius of this strategy is that students' mere ability to explain how they used the word shows you that they are on their way to deeper understanding. The activity also helps students to process these words more deeply and prompts them to increase their usage of rich vocabulary. I use this for vocabulary conferencing or whenever I find time to dialogue with individual students. See Figure 5.6 for a filled-in example of this rubric.

5.6 / Student Self-Assessment

Word	Heard It!	Said It!	Wrote It!	Read It!	Explanation
Curious	✓ ✓ ✓	✓ ✓ ✓ ✓	✓ ✓	✓ ✓	I watched Curious George when I was little. I heard it every day! Now I say it all the time. Like, "Why are you so curious about what I eat?" is what I say to my mom. I also said it in my small group.
Scrumptious	✓ ✓	✓ ✓	✓		My mom said it at dinner because the food was so good. I wrote it in my short story when Tommy ate apple pie.
Drowsy	✓ ✓	✓ ✓ ✓ ✓			I was tired during math class and Mrs. Miller said I looked drowsy. It is one of our vocabulary words, so I say it whenever I am sleepy.
Stingy	✓ ✓ ✓ ✓	✓	✓		My brother says I am stingy because I won't lend him my money. Now I've written it!
Dedicate	✓ ✓	✓	✓		I want to dedicate myself to my work.

PLANNING

If you turn in your lesson plans to the principal weekly or monthly, you are probably including the vocabulary instruction procedures you plan to use throughout the month. Depending on your grade level or content area, you may ordinarily plan for one or two weeks at a time. Now that we've gone through the stages of putting vocabulary into long-term memory—encoding, storage, and retrieval—let's reexamine the planning process.

Decisions, Decisions!

At this point, you may be wondering, "If we are to teach close to 300 Tier 2 words, which ones should we choose, and where do we begin? There are so many!" It may seem overwhelming, but fear not: I have spent much time working with schools to develop vocabulary lists and have devised a straightforward approach to this task. I encourage you to work as a school, department, or grade level to decide which words are going to be on your list, taking these steps:

1. Begin with the high-frequency "critical" terms from the Common Core standards for each grade level (see Figure 5.7), which I discussed in *Teaching the Critical Vocabulary of the Common Core* (2013). I advise adding the words from previous grades to your list along with the words for your grade level. At the very least, pre-assess your students on the previous years' words to make sure they know them.

2. Cross-reference and add words from such sources as Webb's Depth of Knowledge, Bloom's Taxonomy, the Smarter Balanced Tier 2 word list (see http://www.grps.org/images/departments/academics/pdfs/ela/Common_Core_Smarter_Balanced_Word_List.pdf), and Averil Coxhead's list of the top 60 most common academic words (see https://www.vocabulary.com/lists/23710).

3. Finally, examine the words in your own curriculum that students will need to know. Achieve the Core offers a splendid tool called the academic word finder (http://achievethecore.org/page/1027/academic-word-finder-detail-pg) that allows you to enter up to 20,000 words from the text you are using into an application that then picks out the words that need to be studied for your grade level. The application also provides each word's part of speech, which is helpful for English language learners in particular.

5.7 / High-Frequency "Critical" Terms

Grade level	Terms introduced in the Common Core standards
Kindergarten	classify, compare, contrast, describe, distinguish, identify, recognize, retell
1st grade	connections, demonstrate, details, determine, draw, explain, locate, recount, suggest, support
2nd grade	alliteration, comprehend, develop
3rd grade	central idea, explicitly, illustration, organize, point of view, refer, stanza, theme
4th grade	categorize, conclusions, evidence, figurative language, infer, integrate, interpret, metaphor, paraphrase, simile, structure, summarize
5th grade	analyze, interaction
6th grade	argument, articulate, cite, connotative language, delineate, evaluate, mood, tone, trace
7th grade	analogy
8th grade	rhetoric
11th grade	synthesize

There are several points to keep in mind as you create your list. Academic words

- Are crucial to understanding academic texts.
- Appear in all sorts of texts and are highly generalizable.
- Are more likely to appear in written text than to be used in spoken language.
- Often represent subtle or precise ways to say otherwise relatively simple things.
- Require deliberate effort to learn, unlike Tier 1 words.
- Are seldom heavily scaffolded by authors or teachers, unlike Tier 3 words.

Not all highlighted words in your text are necessary or worthy of the time required to teach them. Some factors to consider when identifying academic words to teach include

- *The importance of the word for understanding the text.* What does the word choice bring to the meaning of the text? Precision? Specificity?
- *The general utility of the word.* Is it a word that students are likely to see often in other texts? Does it have multiple meanings? Will it be useful to students in their own writing?

• *Students' prior knowledge of the word and the concept(s) to which it relates.* How does the word relate to other words, ideas, or experiences that students know, are learning, or have gone through? Are there opportunities for grouping words together to enhance student understanding of a concept?

If you work with colleagues, you can develop a more powerful program than if you do it alone. Brainstorming and sharing suggestions and feedback with those who teach the same grade level or content area will generate a more comprehensive list that you can then organize and prioritize. For example, you can decide how many words should be taught in each content area. This collaborative process will eventually yield a somewhat final list (Marzano & Simms, 2013).

Putting It All Together: 20 Steps for Teaching New Vocabulary

First things first. If you are going to use vocabulary notebooks, start right away. Let students get every piece of paper (organizers, index cards, and so on) glued in a composition book or hole-punched for a three-ring binder. Start your vocabulary bag, too. Once you've put these elements in place, it's time to plan your lessons. I tend to think in steps, and the general steps I recommend for teaching new vocabulary look something like the following:

1. Choose your words. They may come from the school's vocabulary word list, the next story or novel, or a new unit.

2. Introduce a word using one of the introductory strategies in Chapter 2. If the text it appears in is a story, you may read the story or have students read it first, unless the new vocabulary will hinder their comprehension. Dramatize the word if possible. For example, let your body droop to illustrate *listless*, or narrow your eyes and jut your chin out to show what *determined* means.

3. Have students repeat the word to ensure proper pronunciation. They are much more likely to use the word if they are confident that they are saying it right!

4. Brainstorm a student-friendly definition. You can have students find the word in the source text and see what definition they come up with through context clues.

5. Provide an illustration that demonstrates the word's meaning. I'm no artist, so I use stick figures, which reassures students that they do not have to draw perfectly when it's their turn.

6. Have students create their own illustrations of the word. They may use symbols.

7. Check for understanding using a formative assessment strategy. Before you go on to the storage step, it's important to catch any misconceptions.

8. Have students pronounce the word again. Now is a perfect time to do this because it signals that we are moving on and this word will soon be "theirs." If you teach ELL students, have the class repeat the word at least three times.

9. Talk about the word's part of speech. As we discussed in Chapter 2, knowing the part of speech will help students identify synonyms, antonyms, and examples. If the word is a true "academic" word, this step will support the fact that these words sound good in writing and speaking.

10. Read aloud some text that the word appears in.

11. Play a synonym game, fill in a synonym circle (see p. 45), or engage in a similar rehearsal activity.

12. Begin to fill in a vocabulary graphic organizer, such as a Frayer Model. Depending on the age of your students, you may want to divide this activity into two sessions so that you can spend more time on each activity.

13. Finish the graphic organizer, rehearse the word, and have students put the organizer into their vocabulary notebook or scrapbook.

14. Game time! Students have done a lot with the word, and it's time for them to test themselves through an engaging rehearsal activity, such as "And the question is . . . ."

15. Participate in another engaging rehearsal activity (e.g., the mystery words strategy, p. 45).

16. Participate in another engaging rehearsal activity (e.g., the picture this strategy, p. 44).

17. Technology time. If you haven't used any technology yet, this is a good time. Have students create a short video using a program like Animoto. Working in pairs, students will create a video that includes the word, examples of the word, and one sentence correctly using the word. You may let students choose which word they want to feature.

18. Popcorn time! Watch the videos and have students discuss and critique each sentence in small groups. Don't tell them, but this is another rehearsal!

19. If the videos featured a variety of words, this is a good time to begin a review like vocabulary association triangles (p. 70). I love these because they

force students to think deeply about the words. Depending on the number of words featured in the videos, students can continue to create these triangles for the next few days.

20. Assess with a review strategy (e.g., I write; you write, p. 71). Students are already in the writing mode, and this exercise is usually fun for them. It will also give you an idea of how well they understand the word. To make sure you give all learners a fair assessment, you may want to use another strategy as well, such as grudge ball (p. 74).

Frequently asked question: Are you teaching only one word at a time?
Answer: Maybe, but probably not. I may introduce one word on Monday, and, as I move through my steps, introduce another word the next day. A common problem that many of us have is a rigid mindset: we cover X words each week, students learn them, we give students a test, and we move on. But these Tier 2 words are "forever" words, and we will need to take more time with some than with others. We need to review words for at least a month after we introduce them. Don't rush yourself or your students.

The following two sections provide sample detailed lesson plans for both the secondary and the elementary level.

Sample One-Week Plan—Secondary Level

This general plan can be used extensively in grades 7–12 by teachers who want to teach academic words to improve students' writing in the content areas or to prepare students for tests like the SAT. This plan covers five words per week, but students may be learning words in other classes.

Day 1. Pre-test. Administer a multiple-choice assessment that has students choose the words' definitions from a list. Allow access to dictionaries or the Internet. After the test, discuss the test answers and the words themselves. (Alternative: instead of a pre-test, give students a self-assessment in which they provide information on their experience with the words; see Figure 5.6 on page 87.)

Day 2. Students write a sentence for each word during the first 5–10 minutes of class. Students then exchange papers and discuss their sentences in pairs or small groups.

Day 3. Again, students begin class by writing sentences using the words. Collect their papers and provide oral or written feedback on their sentences.

Day 4. Picture Day! Students create visuals such as drawings or playdough scenes depicting the word meanings.

Day 5. Administer a formative assessment requiring students to use each word in a sentence.

Students in the upper grades usually enjoy a little friendly competition, so try this activity if you teach at the secondary level. Using chart paper, write the week's words, one per sheet, and post the sheets of paper on the wall. Assign each of your classes a different color, and hand out markers or sticky dots to each class in its respective color. Every time a student uses one of the vocabulary words in class, he or she gets to draw a checkmark or stick a dot on the appropriate sheet. At the end of the week, the class that has accumulated the most marks wins. The prize doesn't need to be big—giving students a token like stickers or extra time to work on something is sufficient. The big win is that they get to brag about their vocabularies!

Every four weeks, give students a major test on 20 words after a few days of review. This post-assessment can be a cloze activity, a multiple-choice assessment, a test requiring them to write sentences using the words, or another format of your choice. To prepare, you can have students engage in peer teaching of mnemonic devices they use to remember the words. The cooperative learning and the drawing from Day 4 help students remember the words well enough that they begin using the words in their writing—thus solidifying their place in long-term memory storage.

Frequently asked question: Does this really work?
Answer: Yes, and students enjoy the challenge. In the upper grades, students have little trouble remembering five words each week. The review and "big test" give their memory networks another boost. Using the words in their writing and across the content areas will further reinforce the words' place in their memories.

Sample Two-Week Plan—Elementary Level

At the elementary level, devising a two-week plan may be more helpful than a one-week plan. Younger students learn words best through engagement strategies such as those used in the following plan.

Day 1. Encoding: Open with a cloze (p. 23). After students complete this exercise, discuss the sentences as a class and go over the words, including pronunciation.

Day 2. Encoding: Visual strategies using technology (p. 31). Have students discuss the word connections that emerge.

Day 3. Encoding: Out of sorts (p. 29).

Day 4. Encoding: Vocabulary anchors (p. 24).

Day 5. Encoding: Miming or acting (p. 26).

Day 6. Storage: Hear it, say it, spell it (p. 45).

Day 7. Storage: Hear it, say it, spell it, rhyme it (p. 45).

Day 8. Storage: Recode, recode, recode (p. 46).

Day 9. Storage: A word before you leave (p. 58).

Day 10. Retrieval: Vocabulary association triangles (p. 70).

Frequently asked question: Ten days for five words doesn't work with my students, whose background knowledge is very limited. What should I do? Teach fewer words? Take more days?

Answer: Experiment with fewer words. Students need a feeling of accomplishment, so let them master fewer words in the same period. Don't worry too much about the 300-word target; teaching 300 words is pointless if the students aren't actually learning the words.

CONCLUSION

Beginning with the end in mind is necessary when explicitly teaching vocabulary. Determining which words you will teach, what strategies you will use, whether students already know the words, and how you will know they know forms a good planning and assessment design. Add to that a reflection on previous vocabulary lesson experiences—the good, the bad, and the ugly—and you will be well on your way to creating your own vocabulary toolbox.

When we talk about building students' vocabulary, we are referring not only to teaching them a large *quantity* of words but also to ensuring that they know these words *well*. According to Beck and colleagues (2013), "knowing a word is not an all-or-nothing proposition: it is not the case that one either knows or does not know a word" (p. 10).

What are *your* vocabulary goals for your students? Some research (Beck et al., 2013) suggests that students need to know words deeply—that it's more important for students to "own" fewer words than to have a superficial knowledge of many words. Others (Biemiller & Boote, 2006) tell us that breadth is better than depth if we want our students to read a wide range of texts.

In my view, a combination of breadth and depth is the ideal. It's also a highly reachable goal when teaching the approximately 300 academic words I recommend. By creating plans for both vocabulary instruction and vocabulary assessment and using a variety of brain-compatible strategies, you will profoundly expand your students' vocabulary and hone their reading comprehension. You will be accelerating learning for some students and closing the achievement gap for others.

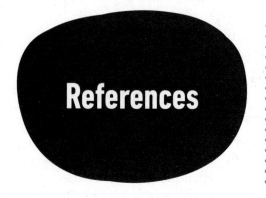

References

Allen, J. (1999). *Words, words, words: Teaching vocabulary in grades 4–12*. Portland, ME: Stenhouse.

Baumann, J. F., Ware, D., & Edwards, E. C. (2007). "Bumping into spicy, tasty words that catch your tongue": A formative experiment on vocabulary instruction. *The Reading Teacher, 61*(2), 108–122.

Beck, I. L., McKeown, M. G., & Kucan, L. (2013). *Bringing words to life: Robust vocabulary instruction* (2nd ed.). New York: Guilford Press.

Berne, J. I., & Blachowicz, C. L. Z. (2008). What reading teachers say about vocabulary instruction: Voices from the classroom. *The Reading Teacher, 62*(4), 314–323.

Biemiller, A., & Boote, C. (2006). An effective method for building meaning vocabulary in primary grades. *Journal of Educational Psychology, 98*(1), 44–62.

Blachowicz, C., Fisher, P., Ogle, D., & Taffe, S. W. (2013). *Teaching academic vocabulary K–8: Effective practices across the curriculum*. New York: Guilford Press.

Cunningham, P. M. (1999). *The teacher's guide to the four blocks*. Greensboro, NC: Carson-Dellosa.

Dehaene, S. (2009). *Reading in the brain: The new science of how we read*. New York: Viking Penguin.

Denner, P. R., Mcginlfy, W. J., & Brown, E. (1989). Effects of story impressions as a pre-reading/writing activity on story comprehension. *Journal of Educational Research, 82*(6).

Dweck, C. (2007). *Mindset: The new psychology of success*. New York: Ballantine.

Dweck, C. (2015, September 22). Commentary: Carol Dweck revisits the "growth mindset." *Education Week, 35*. Retrieved from http://www.edweek.org/ew/articles/2015/09/23/carol-dweck-revisits-the-growth-mindset.html

Feinstein, S. (2013). *Secrets of the teenage brain*. New York: Skyhorse.

Fisher, M. (2016). *Hacking the Common Core.* New York: Times Ten Publications.

Gallagher, J. (2014, June 6). Sleep's memory role discovered. *BBC News.* Retrieved from http://www.bbc.com/news/health-27695144

Glezer, L., Kim, J., Rule, J., Jiang, X., & Riesenhuber, M. (2015, March 25). Adding words to the brain's visual dictionary: Novel word learning selectively sharpens orthographic representations in the VWFA. *Journal of Neuroscience, 35*(12), 4965–4972.

Goleman, D. (1998). *Working with emotional intelligence.* New York: Bantam.

Graves, M. F. (2006). *The vocabulary book: Learning and instruction.* New York: Teachers College Press.

Graves, M. F., August, D., & Mancilla-Martinez, J. (2013). *Teaching vocabulary to English language learners.* New York: Teachers College Press.

Haggard, M. R. (1986, April). The vocabulary self-collection strategy: Using student interest and world knowledge to enhance vocabulary growth. *Journal of Reading,* 634–642. Retrieved from http://darianrivera.weebly.com/uploads/3/8/4/2/38427247/vocab_self-collection.pdf

Hirsch, E. D., Jr. (2013, Winter). A wealth of words. *City Journal.* Retrieved from http://www.city-journal.org/html/wealth-words-13523.html

James, L. (2004). *Meeting Mr. Farmer versus meeting a farmer.* Colorado Springs, CO: Department of Psychology, University of Colorado.

Jensen, E. (2013). *Engaging students with poverty in mind: Practical strategies for raising achievement.* Alexandria, VA: ASCD.

Keeley, P. (2016). *Science formative assessment: Volume 1.* Thousand Oaks, CA: Corwin.

Koprowski, M. (2006, July). Ten good games for recycling vocabulary. *The Internet TESL Journal, XII*(7). Retrieved from http://iteslj.org/Techniques/Koprowski-RecylingVocabulary.html

Lee, H. (1960). *To kill a mockingbird.* London: Heinemann.

López-Barroso, D., Catani, M., Ripollés, P., Dell'Acqua, F., Rodríguez-Fornells, A., & de Diego-Balaguer, R. (2013, August 6). Word learning is mediated by the left arcuate fasciculus. *Proceedings of the National Academy of Sciences of the United States of America, 110*(32), 13168–13173.

Marzano, R. J. (2004). *Building background knowledge for academic achievement: Research on what works in schools.* Alexandria, VA: ASCD.

Marzano, R. J., & Simms, J. A. (2013). *Vocabulary for the Common Core.* Bloomington, IN: Marzano Research.

Moore, D. W., Alvermann, D. E., & Hinchman, K. A. (2000). *Struggling adolescent readers: A collection of teaching strategies.* Newark, DE: International Reading Association.

Mountain, L. (2002). Flip-a-Chip to build vocabulary. *Journal of Adolescent & Adult Literacy, 46*(1), 62–68.

Munoz, L. M. P. (2014, August 23). Coordinating movement, language, and thoughts? An expanded role for the cerebellum. *Journal of Cognitive Neuroscience*. Retrieved from https://www.cogneurosociety.org/cerebellum_ivry_apa

Nagy, W. E., & Anderson, R. C. (1984). How many words are there in printed school English? *Reading Research Quarterly, 19*, 304–330.

Nagy, W. E., & Herman, P. A. (1987). Breadth and depth of vocabulary knowledge: Implications for acquisition and instruction. In M. G. McKeown & M. E. Curtis (Eds.), *The nature of vocabulary acquisition* (pp. 19–35). Hillsdale, NJ: Erlbaum.

Nilsen, A. P., & Nilsen, D. L. F. (2003). A new spin on teaching vocabulary: A source-based approach. *The Reading Teacher, 56*(5), 436–439.

Osborne, M. P. (2009). *Monday with a mad genius*. New York: Random House.

Overturf, B., Montgomery, L., & Smith, M. (2013). *Word nerds*. Portland, ME: Stenhouse.

Padak, N., Newton, E., Rasinski, T., & Newton, R. (2008). Getting to the root of word study: Teaching Latin and Greek word roots in elementary and middle grades. In A. E. Farstrup & S. J. Samuels (Eds.), *What research has to say about vocabulary instruction*. Newark, DE: International Reading Association.

Richek, M. A. (2005). Words are wonderful: Interactive, time-efficient strategies to teach meaning vocabulary. *The Reading Teacher, 58*(5), 414–423.

Richek, M. A., & McTague, B. (2008). Vocabulary strategies for struggling readers. In S. Lenski & J. Lewis (Eds.), *Reading success for struggling adolescent learners* (pp. 189–208). New York: Guilford Press.

Rogers, S., Ludington, J., & Graham, S. (1999). *Motivation and learning*. Evergreen, CO: Peak Learning Systems.

Silver, H. F., Dewing, R. T., & Perini, M. J. (2012). *The core six: Essential strategies for achieving excellence with the Common Core*. Alexandria, VA: ASCD.

Sparks, S. D. (2013, February 5). Students must learn more words, say studies. *Education Week* (Focus On: Literacy). Retrieved from http://www.edweek.org/ew/articles/2013/02/06/20vocabulary_ep.h32.html

Spencer, B., & Guillame, A. (2009). *35 strategies for developing content area vocabulary*. New York: Pearson.

Sprenger, M. (2013). *Teaching the critical vocabulary of the Common Core: 55 words that make or break student understanding*. Alexandria, VA: ASCD.

Sprenger, M. (2014). *Vocab rehab: How do I teach vocabulary effectively with limited time?* Alexandria, VA: ASCD.

Stahl, S. A., & Kapinus, B. (2001). *Word power: What every educator needs to know about teaching vocabulary*. Washington, DC: National Education Association.

Szpunar, K. K., Chan, J. C. K., & McDermott, K. B. (2009). Contextual processing in episodic future thought. *Cerebral Cortex, 19*, 1539–1548.

Thompson, M. C. (2009). *The connection between vocabulary and grammar* [Video]. Unionville, NY: Royal Fireworks Press. Retrieved from https://www.youtube.com/watch?v=KbCPdZ7SCTE

Tileston, D. (2011). *Motivating students*. Paper presented at the Learning and the Brain conference, San Francisco.

Twain, M. (1999). *The wit and wisdom of Mark Twain: A book of quotations*. Mineola, NY: Dover Publications.

Vacca, R. T., Vacca, J. L., & Begoray, D. L. (2005). *Content area reading: Literacy and learning across the curriculum*. Toronto, Canada: Pearson Education.

White, T. G., Graves, M. F., & Slater, W. H. (1990). Growth of reading vocabulary in diverse elementary schools: Decoding and word meaning. *Journal of Educational Psychology, 82*(2), 281–290.

Willis, J. (2014, September 22). Cognitively priming students for learning. *Edutopia*. Retrieved from http://www.edutopia.org/blog/cognitively-priming-students-for-learning-judy-willis

Winters, R. (2001, April). Vocabulary anchors: Building conceptual connections with young readers. *The Reading Teacher, 54*(7), 659–662.

Wolf, M. (2010, June 29). *Our "deep reading" brain: Its digital evolution poses questions*. Cambridge, MA: Nieman Foundation for Journalism.

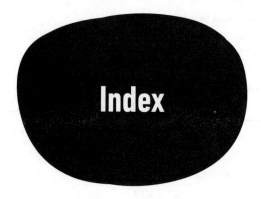

Index

Note: Page references followed by an italicized *f* indicate information contained in figures.

About the Author

Marilee **Sprenger** is a highly regarded educator, presenter, and author who has taught students from prekindergarten through graduate school and has been translating neuroscience research into practice for more than 20 years. The author of 11 books and numerous articles, Marilee is a popular keynote speaker who has engaged audiences throughout the United States and internationally. A member of the American Academy of Neurology, she stays abreast of the latest brain research and is passionate about brain research–based teaching strategies that incorporate differentiated instruction, work with the brain's memory systems, and wire the brain for success. She can be contacted at brainlady@gmail.com or via her website, www.brainlady.com.